UNSUCK LIFE

THE TIPS, TOOLS & TRICKS FOR HOW TO CHANGE WHAT SUCKS, & IMPROVE WHAT DOESN'T

KRISTOFER MENCÁK

Web & social media:
unsucklife.net
facebook.com/unsucklife
youtube.com/@unsucklife
tiktok.com/@unsucklife
pinterest.com/unsucklife
instagram.com/unsucklifenow
twitter.com/unsucklifenow

Copyright © 2022 by Kristofer Mencák

Book Cover by Kristofer Mencák
First edition, 2022

ISBN: 9798361633418 (HardCover)
ISBN: 9798362149024 (Paperback)
Imprint: Independently published

CONTENTS

THE SOLUTION TO OUR PROBLEMS   127

HOW TO MAKE CHANGE EASY   149

YOU CAN DO IT – STARTING NOW   199

INTRODUCTION

Sometimes life sucks, in a big or a small way. What can we do about it? Obviously, we need to unsuck it—make it suck less. That's what this book is about, and I am happy to get the chance to share some of my thoughts about that with you.

The first edition was a spectacular success, not in sales, but it was a test of some ideas I thought would work, and they did. While writing the book, and ever since I published it in 2019, I have tried to follow these ideas.

I am living a life that many people only dream of. Not that I am rich or live a very fancy life. But I am free.

I make enough money to live well, and I do what I want to do for a living, with enough time on my hands to go after other dreams I have. I know change is possible. I know dreams can come true.

It is what it is.
But it doesn't have to be.

And since the ideas in the book worked, I decided I had an obligation to share them with more people. I just needed to change the wording in the book a bit. But when I re-read it, I realized it was very clearly the first attempt at a book. It wasn't as good as I wanted it to be. The writing was sometimes hard to follow, even for me who wrote it! So, I decided to go through it all again. And like most projects in life, it expanded. I added new content, deleted some, and rearranged other content. And I improved my writing.

What you are now reading is an updated version. The goal is that it should help people in the same way it helped me.

I want to give you tools to help change what sucks. I want you to get the courage to go after what you want. And I want you to experience progress because progress is what keeps you going. I probably focus more on finding the dream life, but the tools are the same and can be used for anything, no matter what you want to change or what dream you want to make come true.

Just remember, there's no silver bullet. There's no single key you find or magical potion you can take. Improving life requires work. It's a process, often for a long time.

If you are looking for a quick fix, this book is not for you. Many people are selling quick fixes online. They all work, but not for you. They work for the ones selling them to you. They are the ones making money. They are the ones who have freedom, making money in their sleep.

Instead of wasting time on quick fixes that don't work, we will look at what works. The way to make changes is the same no matter what you want to achieve—if you want to get in shape, become rich, become happy, or do something else.

Since you are reading this book, I believe there's probably something you want to change. But maybe you haven't started yet. That's why we are here.

In addition to all the tools, I also want to give you something more. I want to gift you what people, in general, need most of all—a kick in the ass to get started! So, I am giving it to you now. Can you feel it?

Who am I? Who are You?

I want to make a guess about you. If you are reading this, I guess you are a bit like me. Or at least a bit like what I was like when I started writing this. There's something you want to change. Maybe exercise more, eat healthier, learn something, or you might feel unsure of what you want to do in life. Or maybe there's just a vague feeling that you need to move forward in life—you want to change in some way. You might be happy where you are right now, with what you have achieved so far. But you might also feel you have so much more to give. So much more you want to do. Ideas you want to realize and projects you want to start and finish. In short, there's a disconnect between what you want to do and what you actually do. To me, success is when we have the freedom to do what we want to do. I want you to have that.

If you pick up a non-fiction book about how to succeed in life, you will often read something written by an author who has already made it. They are maybe entrepreneurs, rich, and set for life. And the book tells you about how they made it—their secrets to success.

You will read an intro where they tell you where they live, what kind of house they have, what their perfect family does, and what their ideal life is like. And then, you will learn all their strategies for how you can replicate it.

Well, I am not that person. I am a regular guy. I am not rich. If I could set it, my relationship status with money would be "It's complicated." I still don't know what I will do with the rest of my life. I am still searching. To be honest, it feels like there are too many things I want to do. It's impossible to choose just one. But I know for sure what I don't want to do. I don't want to work the standard 9-5 job for someone else. I want to have the freedom to do what I want.

Anyway, I might be quite a bit like you. And you might be quite a bit like me—a normal person with an everyday life. But in 2014, I made a radical change.

I have a business degree from the Stockholm School of Economics and have worked in online marketing for ten years. My career was progressing fine, and I was interested in digital marketing. I worked in a digital marketing agency with some things I really liked, but also some things that I didn't enjoy as much. Most people can probably relate to that unless they are intensely bored at work.

I have to say it made sense to work there. It seemed safe, and I had a good, fixed income every month. In addition, I liked the job, my boss, and my colleagues. But it wasn't a perfect fit. There was still something inside me that wanted out. Maybe it was more the things I didn't do than the things I did. Perhaps it was that yearning for freedom. There were not enough hours in the day.

One of my passions is dance, and I spend much of my spare time dancing socially. Besides that, I have a creative mind. I love to learn, and I have a lot of ideas. But for a long time, I wasn't much of a doer. No practice, only theory.

A bit by coincidence, I was asked to start teaching dance in Stockholm in 2012. And then I was starting to get requests to travel to teach—first in Sweden, then Europe, and then worldwide. The total workload of a full-time job plus teaching a lot of weekends in faraway places got a bit too much in the end. So, I decided to quit. But I didn't stop dancing. I quit my day job.

I guess it was equal parts craziness and courage, but I felt you only get that kind of chance once in a lifetime—to travel the world doing something you love. I had to take it.

I decided to go all in on dancing and teaching. But under the surface, there was also the feeling that I wanted to do more. And since the teaching was almost only on weekends, this choice would give me time to pursue other things on the weekdays. I had spent far too long thinking about starting different projects. Thinking, not doing. Words, but no action.

Now things are different. I do much more, but it never ends. More ideas come. Even now, after writing three books, there are more books I want to write. There are apps I want to make, courses I want to produce, and product ideas I want to bring to market. So many small dreams I want to make come true. And I believe I have the answer to how I can do that and how *you* can do that too. Creating a positive change in life is not that hard when you know how to do it.

The first edition of this book is a perfect example. It was a project I had started a long time ago. When I was about to the first edition, I thought I had started it a few years before, maybe two or three. But I checked the original file, which was created in October 2013. It meant I had written on it for almost five and a half years.

No. That's a lie. I hadn't been writing on it for that long. I had written maybe 30 pages of text, and then I had simply stopped and left the first 30 pages slowly dying in a folder on my computer. Do you have any projects like that—something you started but never finished? I think we all do.

Anyway, I thought 5,5 years was too slow, so for the first edition, I changed my strategy. Instead of writing a book aimed at other people, I started writing it to myself because I needed it. I wanted to see if the ideas I was writing about in the book would really work—if I could finish the project and publish the book using the ideas. I made it into a proof of concept. Very meta.

I believed it would work, and it did.

Do you have something in your life that you want to change— get a different job, lose some weight, work out more, start following your dreams or maybe just quit smoking? Or is there something you want to do, like learn how to play an instrument, write a book, or create a genius product that will solve a big problem you and many others have? Are you doing something to make it real?

If you are like most people, you are not doing anything about it. Most people don't live their dreams. They give up. Stating it a bit more nicely, they settle. And they use some different excuses for why. Have you ever said or thought of any of this?

- ‣ I don't have enough time.
- ‣ I need some help to start.
- ‣ I just need to learn some more before I start.
- ‣ I want to find the best solution.
- ‣ I would start if it was a bit more realistic.
- ‣ I will start soon when the time is right.
- ‣ I need to hit rock bottom before I change.

Almost all things above could be true. We have a lot of things to do, sometimes we need help with something to be able to start, and the circumstances can always be better.

But the reality is that most people who use that excuse will never get "enough time," they will never search for the help they need to start, and they will never learn "enough." There will always be a better time to start. Like tomorrow. Or Monday. Or next year.

Or will there be? Actually, it will not.

The best time to start was yesterday. The second-best time is today. A dream will forever remain just a dream until you do something about it.

I would be thrilled if you stopped reading now and started working towards your dreams. Because it would mean you have started the journey without wasting time finishing the book! I would be impressed! And what an influential book—accomplishing the goal already in the introduction!

> *"You don't have to see the whole staircase.*
> *Just take the first step."*
> ~ Martin Luther King JR ~

Are you still here? Ok. Maybe I got carried away. I would be happy if you continued reading too.

Even if our rational minds tell us we have reasons not to start, none of the excuses above are good. The thing is, we think that we need to start big. We believe the circumstances need to be right. We want the perfect timing.

We think we need to do that one thing that will change everything. But rarely or ever do big changes come quickly.

Achieving goals in life don't depend on big changes but on small ones. The small things we do every day.

Dreams that come true don't come true out of nowhere. They start materializing when you begin, when you take the first step. Not the perfect move, not the perfect step. Just a step. The first one. That's it.

LIES, LIES, LIES

How Society Fools Us

Let me break something to you already here. You have been fooled, and so have I. But before we dive into how we are deceived, there's something we need to clarify. Life is not a finite game—like a game of chess where we know our opponent, have written rules, a clear goal, and an easy way to determine the winner. We cannot "win" in life.

Life is an infinite game—there are known and unknown players, few fixed rules (even though we do have to follow some laws and conventions), and no clear goal exists. Since we are not playing against anyone else, and the time horizon is endless, there can be no "winner." People can and should have different dreams.

We are just meant to keep playing until life itself takes us out of the game. I believe we are meant to enjoy it as much as possible as long as we are in it.

Since finite and infinite games are so different, we shouldn't approach life with a finite mindset, thinking we can "win" as we do in board games. That could lead to all sorts of problems. If we think of our interactions with others as zero-sum games, where if we win, they will lose, it will affect our professional and private relationships.

As humans, we often seek quick and easy solutions. For that reason, it can be a bit difficult to play with an infinite mindset. We are pattern recognizers. We want to figure out the rules, even if there are none. And then we want to game the system. It's probably an ancient trait that evolution gave us over the millennia.

Recognizing patterns has no doubt served us well. But it's not always the right thing to do. Another thing evolution gave us was short-term thinking when it often makes sense to think long-term.

This search for "rules" makes us vulnerable to an invisible enemy trying to fool us. And this enemy is right here among us. We are even part of the enemy part of "society." It tries to make us believe there *are* some rules in life—rules to follow—rules to become successful. And when we try to follow these rules, our mindset shifts into a finite one. We start thinking about "winning." And it's addictive.

Hitting the jackpot gives us an emotional high. Buying a new expensive car can feel like winning, and it can give a similar rush. Even a promotion to a job we don't want can feel like "winning". Think about that last sentence a bit. We hear the word "promotion" and think it's "winning". But if it's a job we don't want, it can't be "winning," can it?

Adopting a finite mindset in the infinite game of life can be tempting. This is how we fool ourselves. We keep searching for those "wins," and when we do that, we get stuck in a hamster wheel.

Our chances to enjoy life are better if we play with the right mindset. When we understand that life is an infinite game, it will be easier to make decisions that will make us happy. When we don't desperately try to follow the "rules" of how we should live to "win." And when we don't play for the temporary emotional highs, but play more long term, with infinite time horizons. And when we play to enjoy ourselves.

That's key—if we want to be happier, we must do more things that make us happy.

The Wrong Recipe for Success

From the day we start school, and sometimes even earlier, we are told the rules for how to succeed in life. A whole system is built around it, and I am sure you already know it. You have been brainwashed, just like me.

We learn that we must study hard and get good grades to get into a good university. Then we must study hard again and get good grades, so we can get a good job. Finally, we must advance in our careers every now and then and make a lot of money. So that's what most people try to do.

When we follow this system, we go on like this for maybe 40 years as if we are on autopilot, and then when we retire, we can finally relax and do the things we love. We can finally enjoy life a bit more. If we are still in good health.

We think this is what we want. We believe this is what *we* want. But is it really? Is it our own little voice in our head telling us this. Is it our own internal compass that points us in this direction? Or is it something we just blindly follow because it is generally accepted as "truth"?

I'd rather be poor and have fun than be rich and bored. In addition, striving for more money is never-ending. We can always have more; therefore, we will never have enough. We will never be satisfied. This was never a good plan, and it's even worse now.

People are different—we like different things, think differently, and have different talents and aspirations. So, having the same plan as everyone else can't be a good plan.

Some people are good at working with their hands. Others are better with their heads. Some people need stability and prefer routine work—they feel good doing more or less the same thing every day. Others thrive on changes and challenges. We are created to have different talents and to be drawn to different things, so why should we follow the same path? Why should we all follow the same standardized way of living our lives?

> *"Your time is limited, so don't waste it*
> *living someone else's life."*
> ~ Steve Jobs ~

Most people seem to have the kind of career expected from them. Often something that they thought would please their parents or impress their friends. Or something that's generally appreciated in the society they live. They were made to believe it was right for them. It seemed like the right thing to do. Or they didn't think it was right for them, but they valued other people's opinions more than their own. Society is not excelling at teaching people how to think for themselves or listen to their dreams and aspirations. So, these people end up doing something that pays the bills. Something they can stand. Barely. Not something they love. And many of them end up making just enough money.

Why? Because when you don't love what you do, it's hard to do it with passion. And without that, it's hard to put in that extra that makes the work stand out. And no one will pay extra for it if it doesn't stand out—what it would be worth if it was brilliant, done with passion.

A few others somehow manage to do great work anyway, and make good money, despite not loving what they do. They advance fast in their careers and go fast forward. But...

What good is going fast if you're going in the wrong direction?

Most companies have some corporate objectives stated in their yearly report. When we work for a company, this is what we work for. That's what we are spending our time on. Do you know what you are working for? How do these objectives feel? Does "maximize shareholder value" sound like a worthy purpose? Something worth dedicating your life to? To me, it doesn't. But that's the primary objective of many companies, and by extension also their staff's objective, when they are at work, which is most of their life.

> *"If your success is not on your own terms, if it looks good to the world but does not feel good in your heart, it's not success at all."*
> ~ Anna Quindlen ~

I would guess around 80 % of all people don't really enjoy their work. They don't really like Mondays. On Sunday, they get anxious just thinking about Monday. Are you one of them?

To make matters worse, this plan where we follow society's recipe for success is even worse now. Times are changing. What previously was a safe job, and a safe plan is not safe anymore.

The world is now truly global. Markets for pretty much everything are global. Competition is tougher than ever.

Companies charging forward on autopilot, doing things "the way we do things here," live a dangerous life. Global markets and tougher competition mean some of them are bound to fail. And this means that if we work in a company that can't face the competition, we might be without our job any day.

In addition, technology changes fast. What was state of the art yesterday could become obsolete today. Some entire industries are bound to fail. And with them, a lot of people will lose their jobs. Most of their skills and what they know could become useless. So, on an individual level, mindlessly doing the same things every day doesn't work in this world anymore.

What was considered safe is not safe anymore. We can never be sure to keep our jobs as long as we are employed by someone else. Very few companies or industries are moving towards more full-time staff. Most are cutting back, hiring more temp workers, or automating. And this is especially true for lower-skill positions.

In conclusion, today we can "fail" even when we choose the traditionally relatively safe path prescribed by society. As if having a job that we don't even like isn't failure enough.

There are no guarantees in life. Well-educated people can fail, and non-educated can succeed.

When there's no guarantee, the smartest thing we can do is listen to our hearts, follow our feelings, and try to achieve our dreams. Do something that we love. It will make us happier. And being happy is never wrong.

Tougher competition than ever is the downside of global markets. But global markets also mean there are a million new possibilities. The market for our specific skills is also international, and we can sell them worldwide.

There's something that I have believed for a long time, and I have repeated it to many friends over the years:

If you love something, you will do it a lot. If you do it a lot, you will become good. And when you are good, you can make money.

Don't you instinctively feel that it's true? When we look around, we see so many examples of it. I believe that if we do something long enough, we cannot help but improve. And soon enough, we are so good we are considered an "expert." And when other people view us as an expert, we can make money.

Come to think of it, it's not even necessary to make a lot of money. We don't need that much to survive. If we are happy with what we do, it's worth more than having a lot of money.

> *"Trying to be someone else is a waste*
> *of the person you are."*
> ~ Curt Kobain ~

It can be tricky, I agree. But it's worth it. Doing things that make us happy daily is the best way to live this life. The alternative hoping that someday in the future, we will become happy if we follow what everyone else is doing—is not the best way. We must choose wisely.

Consumerism

The first big lie is mostly about income—how we make money. The second big lie is on the other end—about how we spend and what we spend on. As a rule, we can reduce it to this:

"We buy things we don't need with money we don't have to impress people we don't like."

This quote, with slight variations, has been attributed to several people, some real and some fictional. Tyler Durden in the movie Fight Club, Will Smith, and Dave Ramsey have all said something similar. The earliest quote I have found along these lines was from the early twentieth century, made by a comedian called Will Rogers.

We are constantly fed the lie that we must consume. We must buy stuff. New stuff. The next thing. More and more, and faster and faster. We are told what to buy to become more popular, successful, happy, or healthy.

In the end, we buy a lot of things that we don't need. Stuff that stays in the wardrobe or a drawer somewhere. And it's not just the fact that we don't need them. We also buy things to impress other people. We purchase specific brands and spend much more than what we would have spent if we only paid for the functionality of what we buy.

I think part of this is evolutionary. We were hunter-gatherers. We like to gather things. We want to bring home the "prey." But I also think this consumption somehow makes us feel better, at least temporarily. Maybe it makes up for our own insecurities. Perhaps we use this consumption as a way to compare ourselves to other people. To feel equal or better.

> *"Showing off is the fool's idea of glory."*
> ~ Bruce Lee ~

But truth be told, we don't even care much about most of these people we try to impress. The people we care about, the ones who care about us, are not impressed by the stuff we buy anyway.

Popularity, health, success, and happiness don't come from consumption. Those are all things money can't buy.

Maybe even worse, some of the stuff we buy is bad for us and our health. We are fooled into consuming foods and drinks that make us fat and unhealthy. Some products have been specifically developed to make us hooked on them. Sugar is addictive. We get in bad shape. We get lousy health, and then endless commercials on TV sell us drugs that might decrease the symptoms but will never eliminate the root cause.

To make matters even worse, many of these things we buy are bought with money we haven't earned yet. We use credit. The financial markets tell us it's ok. We can pay later because it's good for them. That way, they make more money in the end. But it's not good for us. This is the reason average personal debt is higher than ever before.

With this debt we accumulate and the interest we must pay on it, we become even more stuck in the rat race. We get trapped in the lies we have been told. It makes it much harder to break free. It contributes to our fear of leaving this path we were told to follow. We are in debt. We need to pay interest. So, we must make money and stay in that fixed-income "safe" job.

> *"A man in debt is so far a slave."*
> ~ Ralph Waldo Emerson ~

We pick a career we don't want to be able to buy things we don't need, with money we don't yet have, to impress people we don't like.

The Big Break & Quick Fixes

Are you dreaming of The Big Break—the stroke of luck that will resolve all your problems? I am sorry, but it will not happen. What about that magic pill that will transform your body in 10 days? Sorry, but it doesn't exist. Yes, there are ways to lose weight and get a physically fit and healthy body, but not in 10 days. Not even in 30 days if you are in bad shape.

If you are waiting to win the lottery—good luck! The odds of winning enough money to be financially independent for the rest of your life are one in 100 million. If you want those odds for the chance to get a good life—go ahead and take a bet!

Advertisers like to make us believe there's a chance, or maybe even very likely, that we will get that breakthrough. They want to sell us the idea that it will be easy if we only get what they sell. But the truth is not on their side.

There's no quick fix. If it sounds too good to be true, it usually is. Becoming rich, happy, or healthy is not an event. It's a process. First, you sow, then you cultivate, and then you harvest. Only after a lot of work can you reap the rewards. That's life. No shortcuts. If you only think short term, you will not get long-term results.

There's a reason many people who win a lot of money soon find themselves to be just as poor again. Why? They have won this massive amount of money by a stroke of luck, but they don't cultivate it well. They don't know how to make money grow. They know how to spend, so they lose it and end up right where they started.

It's the same with crash diets, which we complete in 10 days or 30 days. When we see someone in great shape, we can bet they did not achieve it in 10 days. They didn't go on any diet. The idea that we can permanently change our bodies with a temporary change in diet is fundamentally flawed. Long-term results come from long-term thinking, determination, and consistency.

If there's one thing we need to understand, it's this: it's the cultivation, the process, and how consistent we are over time that creates results. The things we do every day will have a tremendous effect over time. These are the things that really have the power to change our lives. Little by little. Day by day.

Any successful person knows that nothing comes for free. It takes time and effort, but time can be our friend.

Without time, no health improvement, no compound interest in our savings, no better body, no personal development, and no change in happiness. It's just over time that results can grow enough to really show. But when we put in the effort, time is our best friend.

We have to take care though because time doesn't care about us. It can also be our enemy. If we choose to do the wrong things in life, even if it's just tiny things, then time will work against us and amplify it over time.

We seem to go through life repeating the same things over and over again. We wake up, do a quick morning routine, have breakfast, go to work, have lunch, work some more, eat dinner, and then do something in the evening before it's time to sleep. But there are slight differences in what we do—differences in how our routines look, differences in what we do just after waking up, and differences in what we have for breakfast. In what we do on the way to work. In how we do our work. If we put a workout in or not. Throughout the day, small choices make a big difference over time.

And they will all work against us if they are the wrong ones. They will accumulate and multiply, and sooner or later, we will pay the price.

Or we will reap the rewards if the choices are good. Because the compounding effect is "on" all the time. It will work for us or against us. It's up to us to make a choice.

Every day you can set yourself on a new path. Every moment you can give yourself a new direction. In a way, it's easy because it's just one small decision at that very moment. The decision isn't to eat healthy for the rest of your life. It's just this meal. This one time. And then you repeat that small decision as often as you can.

Little by little, day by day, life will improve if we decide to make some better decisions every day. We need to make that choice. We need to act. We need to be consistent. Then and only then will time reward us.

It will not look like much at first. Only with time will the compound effect reveal itself. But if we stay with it long enough, we will be beautifully rewarded. Remember, there are no quick fixes.

The Limits of Life

Talking about time, by the way. Do you think you have enough? Well, you might, and you might not. Can you know for sure what you will do tomorrow or a year from now? Or when you retire? No, you can't. Any moment life can end. Or if we are less dramatic—at any moment, life can change, and what we plan to do in a year or five years is no longer possible.

"Waste your money and you're only out of money, but waste your time and you've lost part of your life."
~ Michael LeBoeuf ~

We take a considerable risk when we keep dreaming of those things we love to do and plan to do when we are retired and have time. Things can change fast. And even if nothing dramatic happens, we might still not be able to enjoy them if we simply don't take care of our health.

When we are young, we have time and health, but we usually don't have much money. When we are a bit older, we typically still have health and more money, but we don't have much time.

And when we get old, we usually have money and time, but quite often, we don't have health.

When you gamble with time, you go all in, because all you really have is now. Time wasted is time lost. And you can never get it back.

It's a mistake to think we have enough time to do everything. We might be doing the wrong things now. We might realize there wasn't enough time to do what was truly important. It will give us regrets, and no one wants that.

"We have two lives, and the second begins when we realize we only have one."
~ Confucius ~

But it's possible to live in another way. It's possible to change. Have you ever heard about someone who was really close to death, maybe someone who was battling some deadly disease or suffered a severe accident? They were on the edge between life and death and survived. What do they always say? They have learned to take life day by day and live here and now. They do what they like to do. They try to live their dreams. They make sure to spend time with family and friends. They have learned to appreciate life much more, and many of them claim that their lives have been made fuller by the experience. Maybe we can learn something from them.

They learned from the experience of being close to death. They realized, in an intense way, that they will not live forever. They understood that the only time that matters is now. If we want to be sure to do something, we must do it now. We cannot postpone living until tomorrow or next year because we don't know if we will experience it.

Life is just a lot of moments. It exists only right now. If you make your moments matter, you make your life matter.

So, we have to take care. Do things we enjoy. Things that make us feel alive. We must learn to say no to whatever is not enjoyable. It's not always easy, but it's worth it. Because if we say yes to everything, we will start resenting the people we say yes to, we will do a lousy job at work we wish we had said no to, and in the end, it's time wasted. Energy wasted that we could have used on something we enjoy—something that would make our life matter.

"A 'No' uttered from the deepest conviction is better than a 'Yes' merely uttered to please, or worse, to avoid trouble."
~ Mahatma Gandhi ~

Every moment is full of opportunities. We have some time—we don't know how long—and we also have some dreams. If we assume we have just one life, how come we are not running like crazy chasing them? Are we happy to spend our time on "stand by"? Spending life on average, waiting to have time to live? I think not. I believe we have to live our lives to the fullest. Every day.

But we need to be smart about it. We need to figure out what living to the fullest means for us.

Since we can never be sure how long we have, we must be smart and live now. At the same time, we also need to live in a way so that we are not creating problems for ourselves in the future. What we do right here and now determines our level of joy at the moment. But it also shapes our future—our possibilities to enjoy the future.

Everything you do sets you on a new path toward the future. It gives you a slightly different direction. And you can change that direction at any moment. Where are you heading?

So, what can we do to find the balance between living now while we are still thinking about the future?

First, I believe we need to live with passion. We need to dedicate most of our time to things we love that give us meaning because otherwise, our time here is not lived to the fullest.

Second, we need to live in a way that doesn't limit our possibilities of having a good life in the future. Even if I love the taste of a good brownie, I can't spend every waking hour eating brownies in front of the TV because if I do, soon, that will be all I can do. I will not be able to get off the sofa. In the same way, no matter how nice it is to be able to spend money, we also need to think about retirement a bit. We don't want to live in the street when we are old.

And third, if we really want to maximize our life, we must try to live in a way that gives us a chance at a longer and healthier life. Better health means we can enjoy each moment more, and we will also live for longer. The body is our tool to be able to experience the joys of life. If the body is out of shape, we cannot enjoy life as well anymore.

The same goes for our mind. If we don't use it, we lose it. We should strive for a longer health span and a longer lifespan for both body and mind. Life is not long enough to waste it being miserable.

Imagined Expectations

Maybe this one is not quite a lie. It's not like we are being told this. Perhaps it's more like something we have created in our heads and believe to be true. It's about expectations. It's about the disconnect between what we think others expect from us and what they really want.

I know a lot of people feel stuck. With their jobs. With their studies. With their lives. They have entered a road of no return. Or at least that's what it feels like. They might have a job they don't like or maybe have a marriage they don't enjoy. Or they are studying something that they don't really think is interesting. On a more general level, there's something in life that they don't like, but they feel like it's impossible to change. Why is that? I think that quite often, it's because they fear what other people will think.

> *"I'm not in this world to live up to your expectations and you're not in this world to live up to mine."*
> ~ Bruce Lee ~

It's common to feel pressure from our environment, sometimes from our nearest and dearest. We might feel it from our parents. We might feel it from our life partner. We might feel it from our friends or social circles. We think they expect us to have a specific career. Or that we should have a perfect marriage. We believe they want to see us continue on our road. We might be struggling on that road, but we continue no matter how much we suffer. We might even pretend to be happy just because we want to please them. We want to fit in and often follow what *we* think *they* want.

Yes, they might give their opinions. They might say that they want us to do this and that. They might advise us to do something because they want what *they* believe is good for us. And maybe they think that we want it too. But this is the thing—in most cases, this is not what they want. They mean well, but they don't realize they also bought into the lies.

The people around you don't want you to work in any specific area. They don't expect you to have a specific career. They don't want a particular type of partner for you. They don't want you to suffer, and they don't want you to pretend anything. If they give you their opinion and you ask them the question "why" repeatedly, you will find what they really want: They just want you to be happy.

There really isn't much more than that. That's what they want. What they say to you is just what *they* somehow believe would make *you* happy. But if you dig deep, what they want is your happiness.

Of course, if you choose to have a family, you will probably need to contribute to family finances. And there are other expectations too. But exactly *how* you contribute to those finances is hardly their biggest concern. Precisely *what* you do for a living is not their biggest concern unless it's something illegal.

Parents don't want their son or daughter to suffer in a bad marriage, no matter if it looks like it was a match made in heaven or how good and happy it looks from the outside. They want you to be with someone you genuinely love.

Your life partner doesn't want you to work as a CEO or any other position and be miserable, not taking care of your health and running the risk of a heart attack by age 54. They want you to do something you love. They want you to achieve your life dreams.

Ironically, the best way for you to make your family and friends happy is to become happy yourself. And you don't become happy trying to make them happy.

The weird thing is that they might not even be aware of this problem they create. But this is only because they also believe the lies that there's a right way of living life. They have also been fooled into believing it, and they might show it if you choose to change. They might try to resist your change. They might try to talk you out of it. Just remember that they do this because they want you to be happy, and this is what they believe will make that happen. When you follow your heart, do what you love, and become happy as a result, they will see it and understand you did the right thing. Maybe they too will realize what truly matters.

The truth is the people who really care about you don't care about precisely how you live your life. They just want you to be happy. And if you are, they are.

Growing Up

I admire kids. They have so many qualities we adults seem to miss. We grow out of them. Or we are forced to grow out of them. We are told to "grow up," and we do. We start taking responsibility. We begin to act like adults in every way possible. I think that's a mistake. Kids have so many qualities we should keep. Maybe we should try to stay more like a child in many ways.

> *"Every child is an artist. The problem is how to remain an artist once he grows up."*
> ~ Pablo Picasso ~

Kids are honest. Sometimes they are scary honest. Even embarrassingly honest.

But we forgive them for it. They are just kids, and honesty is good. I think we should follow their example and be more honest, also to ourselves. Truth is good. Don't fool yourself. Don't hide what you feel. Be more honest with yourself and others, and life will be better.

Kids are curious in both big and small ways. They want to discover the world, and they want to see what's in your underwear. They ask questions. They want to know. When we stop asking so many questions, we also stop learning. Keep asking. Stay curious.

Kids play. And they can play with anything—anything can be a toy. A cell phone mini tripod is a space rocket. Everything is interesting. It doesn't take much to make them have fun. Playing is how they learn about the world and how to interact with it. And with every play, they develop. Keep playing, and you keep developing.

Kids are incredibly creative. They build, draw, invent, and they create. Creativity is what drives the world forward. Negativity and judgment are what kill it. Don't let anyone kill yours.

Kids have a great imagination. They see the possibilities. Four lines on paper is a boat. Let your imagination loose and keep looking for possibilities.

> *"Your imagination is everything. It is the*
> *preview of life's coming attractions."*
> ~ Albert Einstein ~

Kids are easily amused. Anything can cause a laugh—an accident, a facial expression, even something as simple as a sound. Take life a bit easier and enjoy the small things.

Kids are not afraid to dream of becoming an astronaut, a superhero, or something equally ambitious. Interestingly, few dream of becoming accountants, lawyers, and management consultants. Can that tell us something? Dream big and keep your dreams alive.

> *"A goal is not always meant to be reached, it often serves simply as something to aim at."*
> ~ Bruce Lee ~

Kids know what they want, and they manifest it. If they are sad, they show it. If they want to do something, they show it. And if they don't want to, they show it too. They don't say yes to something they don't wish to do just to please us. Know what you want and do what you can to get it. But maybe without throwing a tantrum.

Kids don't give up. They try to walk and fall. They try again and fall. They try again, and they walk. And they do this with everything. Rolling over to the belly. Crawling. Walking. Running. Jumping. Keep developing, and don't give up.

For kids, everything is possible, and I believe we should try to keep that mentality. Yes, maybe we should grow up in some respects. Take responsibility for our lives. But we probably shouldn't grow up in every possible way. We should keep some traits that kids have. Be honest, also to ourselves. Stay curious. Keep playing. We shouldn't let anyone kill our creativity. Our imagination should be free, we should enjoy the small things, and we should keep dreams alive. Know what you want and go after it. And don't give up. Everything is possible.

Living the Lies

Why do we live these lies? Why do we try to follow the "rules" and try to win in the game of life? Partly because we have been made to believe them. They are so ingrained in us that we don't question them, even if we feel something isn't right.

But we also live these lies because we chose the path of least resistance.

We don't always choose the least resistance in terms of the amount of work we have to do. A lot of people literally work their asses off. But then we choose the path of least resistance from society. We choose what we feel breaks fewer expectations.

So, what happens when we live these lies? Well, our life will be like most people's. It can be pretty comfortable in many ways. We might be reasonably successful and reasonably well off. But it's also likely our life will be very much like the people who hate Mondays and can't wait for Friday. Like the people who live empty lives and spend their money on useless stuff to impress others. Like the people constantly trying to search for the quick fix, whether it's a magical diet pill or some form of lottery. We might constantly be adjusting our life to what we think others expect from us. Living someone else's life. And we might feel we are always with the nose just above the surface since we don't love what we do and must constantly struggle.

We might still have dreams. But we will not do anything to reach them. We don't dare. We are waiting for something to happen. Waiting for our chance to come. We might not even know for what, but we are waiting. Postponing life. And then, someday, it will be too late. Then we will regret everything we didn't do—the things we didn't even try.

Or we can decide that we want to give ourselves a chance. We want to give our life a chance. To live it fully, without regrets.

What has passed doesn't matter. Where you are right now also doesn't matter. It's what you do at this moment that matters. And at every moment from now on. Either you do something to improve life, or you don't. What do you think you deserve?

> *"Most of us go to our graves with our music still inside us, unplayed."*
> ~ Oliver Wendell Holmes ~

Imagine that. I wouldn't want to feel I have wasted my life. I believe neither would you. All it takes to avoid regrets is to stop dreaming and start doing something. Really give it a try, and you will have no regrets. Because if you tried, there's nothing to regret.

*"Only put off until tomorrow what you are
willing to die having left undone."*
~ Pablo Picasso ~

What's Important in Life?

You would think that humans figured life out already, right? I mean, people go to work, advance their careers to get their house and car, have their families, and go on vacations. And then they work some more to buy more things and go on slightly better holidays or maybe get a second car, a boat, or a summer house. It's the prescribed way of living, so doesn't it make sense to go along? I mean, everybody does it, right?

To be honest. I doubt it. What's important in life? I mean, *really* important? Is it money? Family? Relationships? Is it being true to ourselves? We only live once, so what we choose to do with our time is incredibly important.

I think most people wouldn't say their work is what's most important. It's hardly the meaning of life. A lot of people don't even like their work.

*"Let's be honest. It's not Mondays
that suck. It's your job!"*

I have to say it's true. If you don't like Mondays, it's not because Mondays are inherently worse than any other day. It's not that bad things happen on Mondays. No, it's because

Monday is the first day of the week and most people must go to work again. It starts their five days of suffering before they are "free" again on Friday afternoon.

If Sunday afternoons and evenings are spent in anxiety over Monday, it's time to do something about it.

But what? And how? Maybe start doing something else on the side of the day job. Build a business on the side. Or start looking for another job that would be more enjoyable. Or quit straight away if it's possible.

I believe we should all find purpose and passion in what we do because it makes us happier. When we are happier, our close ones will be happier. When they are happier, they will, in turn, affect everyone around them. The circle of happiness will grow. And if enough people feel purpose, I believe we will have a better world, more focused on what's really important.

Have you ever heard of Bronnie Ware? She was an Australian nurse who worked in palliative care, caring for people during the last 12 weeks of their lives. During this care, she collected some of their stories, and she also did a survey among them. She was curious to discover their biggest regrets in life after gaining all the wisdom that a long life gives.

So here they are—the biggest regrets among older people when they are about to die:

I wish I had the courage to live a life true to myself, not the life others expected of me.

This was the most common regret. People didn't follow their own hearts in life. Instead, they tried to live up to other people's expectations. This is about you and me. I have to live *my* life as *I* want. I must follow *my* own dreams and passions. And you have to live *your* life as *you* want. You must follow *your* own dreams and passions.

We are often told what to do: "Study hard and get a good job." We fall for the first lie. Through our different school systems and higher education, no one ever mentions passion. And no mention of happiness that I can remember of. I have never taken a course on how to become happy.

Instead, it's assumed happiness will follow the "good job," but what "good" really means in this expression is "well paid."

The problem is that money doesn't buy happiness. Making a lot of money doesn't lead to happiness. There are a lot of people considered successful who are profoundly unhappy.

I would rather say that happiness leads to success. First, I think being happy *is* a success. And secondly, what society considers success often comes as a consequence of being great at what we do. And we become great when we love what we do because we do it a lot.

Yes, it's easier to live when we have money. It can solve a lot of small and big problems. But having money doesn't mean we become happy. Sometimes the opposite happens. Money might even lead people astray towards a more materialistic lifestyle with less meaning. People start searching for "happiness" through temporary pleasures, buying things. But the constant desire for something more or something else doesn't lead to happiness. Actually, the opposite is true.

It's when we don't desire something else that we are happy. If we live the way we think others expect from us and not the way we want to, we will always feel this desire for something else. We will always feel we don't have the job we should have. We will long be in a different place and live another way. We will not be happy. And if we keep living like that, we will regret it. Remember, no one will ever thank you for holding back who you really are.

> *"If you don't start building your dream, someone else will hire you to build theirs."*

Most people who are working for someone else in a company are not building their own dreams. If we don't make courageous choices in life, no one else will make them for us either. Taking charge of life is the only way. Taking responsibility to do what we want.

I wish I hadn't worked so hard.

The second most common regret was something that men especially had—every one of them! But I am sure this will change, and not for the better. I think there's a generational difference.

The people who answered this survey were from a different generation and lived in other times. I believe that men will still feel this way 20, 30, or 40 years from now, but just as many women will feel the same unless something dramatically changes. In many societies, women pursue careers just as much as men do, putting as much work in as men do.

There are several important conclusions we can draw from this regret. The first and most apparent is that these people spent too many hours working. They didn't have enough time for other important things. The second is that maybe they felt they worked so hard because they didn't like the job. If they had loved their job, maybe it wouldn't have felt like work the same way? Perhaps they would have enjoyed it more? Maybe they would have felt it was more about fulfilling a purpose or a dream? And therefore, they wouldn't regret it as much. So, we are back to the number one regret about being truer to ourselves.

Yet another conclusion could be this: maybe the real regret was on the flip side of the coin—working so much led to not spending enough time with family and friends. Working hard is not that bad in and by itself. But the consequences might be—if we feel that we spend our years the wrong way. That's what we regret in the end.

I wish I'd had the courage to express my feelings.

This was the third most common regret. A lot of people held their feelings back to keep peace with others. Of course, if we don't dare to show or express what we feel, we will never be able to change anything for the better. Holding back will never help change a situation we dislike. It will also affect us mentally. Just the action of expressing a feeling can be a relief, even if it doesn't create any real change. It has been proven that we don't even have to tell anyone what we feel. It can be enough to write it down in a diary, and we will feel better.

There are so many ways expressing our feelings can help in life. I am sure there are more people who, like me, have been afraid to express feelings of love for fear of rejection. When we have the courage, it can help us get more peace of mind. We might feel better just letting it out. But in many cases, it can also help change a situation we don't like.

I wish I had stayed in touch with my friends.

The fourth most common regret was not staying in touch with friends. Many people didn't understand the benefits of having good friends until it was too late. Once again, I think we are a bit back to the job issue, and the life we feel is expected. We believe we must run through life, progress in our careers, and chase promotions. And since time is limited, the more time we spend on the job and chasing promotions, the less time we have to stay in touch with friends. If we don't take care of our friends, sooner or later, they are gone.

If we want to live a long and happy life, one of the most essential ingredients is keeping good relationships alive. Good relationships prolong both life and health. We will be happier and actually live longer.

I wish that I had let myself be happier.

The last of the biggest regrets was about letting oneself be happier. Life is full of choices. Even happiness can be a choice. Quite often, we take the path of least resistance. We choose what feels easy and comfortable. Often things that don't change the current situation too much. Instead of trying to become happy, people pretend to be content with what they have in life. They adapt who they are to fit the image of what they think people expect. But pretending to be happy is not the same as being happy.

Making a radical change in life is not easy. It requires a lot of courage. Taking the road less traveled is scary, and quite often, we are met with resistance when we break expectations. It's not easy to follow our heart and go for it. But we must if we want to allow ourselves to be happy.

One Life

We have only one life, and it's pretty short. One chance. No rehearsal. No re-run. And no possibility of pressing "pause." It keeps going while we try to figure out what we want and while we dream and talk about what we want but are too afraid to act. So, we need to get it into our heads that we only have one chance.

- What's really important in your life?
- What would you never want to stop doing?
- What's not really contributing to your life?
- What's essential in your life, but not necessary that you do yourself?

We need to make sure to get our priorities right and do what we want to do. When we skip doing what doesn't contribute, we will free up time to do more important things. And what we don't really need to do ourselves, we can let someone else do if they can do it just as well. Then we get even more time on our hands.

It's not what you did that you regret. It's what you didn't do—the things you wanted to say or do but didn't.

So, what do you want to do? What do you dream of? You need to have some goals in this infinite game of life. You need to have something to strive for. Something that makes you feel alive.

What prevents regrets is that we try. If we fail, it doesn't matter because, in the end, we know that we gave it a shot. It's when we don't even try that we get regrets.

WHAT DO YOU WANT?

Awareness

It's never enough to raise the hand and say, "I want more in life." We must figure out what's wrong. And we have to figure out what we want. We all have some dreams in life. There are some things we want to achieve. And maybe some things we want to change. Knowing where we are and what we want will give us an idea of what and how much we need to change.

So, what are we not happy about? Is it about health? Weight? Finances? Smoking? Exercise? Or is it more related to what we do to make a living? Do we see our work as just a job, making us money? Do we see it as a career, a way of advancing salary, title, or power? Or do we see it as a calling? Is it filled at least partially with something that gives us meaning? How do we feel about it?

> *"Discontent is the first necessity of progress."*
> ~ Thomas A. Edison ~

Of course, when life is pure hell, most people will change something. We will take action. But if we are not yet living pure hell—if our life is tolerable—we might be inventing excuses as to why we don't do anything about it.

A lot of people feel the balance is not good. They are not focusing on the right things in life, but they are not sure what they want and are not confident enough in the alternatives.

Some might want to change, but their fear is too powerful. So, they wait. Maybe they are waiting for a promotion, a raise, or the project from hell to be over. But will the unhappiness really go away once that happens? Some people will convince themselves it will. But quite often, it won't. Waiting might result in a minor change, making it better or worse. In reality, it's usually just more of the same. More of what wasn't very good to begin with.

Other people will start to change when they feel just a little bit uncomfortable, a little bit unhappy, no matter if it's about their weight or if it's about what they do in life.

If you are unhappy at work, what do you get out of it besides getting paid? Do you feel joy in what you do? Do you feel creativity? Do you feel you are being challenged? Do you feel satisfaction? Do you feel progress? Do you feel appreciated? Do you feel you make a difference in the world?

What likely would happen if you decided to change? What's the worst that could happen? And if that worst thing happened, what would it mean? Would it be the end of the world? Or how bad would it be? And for how long would it last?

How likely is this worst-case scenario? What other outcomes could you imagine, and how likely are they? What if you achieved your wildest dream? How happy would that make you?

When we feel it's impossible to make a radical change, maybe it's possible to change something to make us feel better about it, to make us feel more alive? Can we work on something else, on the side, that gives us that feeling?

When we conclude that we are far from where we want to be, we need to see what has taken us there. The saying goes: "The definition of insanity is doing the same thing over and over and expecting different results." The quality of life depends a lot on the quality of what we do day to day.

If you are unhappy with life, doing more of the same will not solve anything. Try something else. Turn off the autopilot and take control.

Sometimes we have made a one-time decision that took us to where we are, which wasn't right. It set us on the wrong path. Or it might have been small everyday choices that accumulated over time and led us to where we are.

> *"If you do not change direction, you may end up where you are heading."*
> ~ Lao Tzu ~

So, we need to figure out what got us to that place and then make some changes. Was it because we listened too much to other people and not enough to our hearts? Is it reckless spending? Is it constant sipping on sugar-filled soft drinks? Is it spending all our spare time in front of the TV? Is it blaming others for failures and not taking responsibility? Is it using excuses to save ourselves from the effort? Or is it just plain fear of the unknown?

Once we know where we are, how we feel about it, and how we got there, we also have an idea of what we need to change. When it comes to health, weight, finances, and similar, it's easier to figure out. When it comes to our purpose in life, it can be more challenging.

Start Tracking

The best way to get a reality check is to start tracking. We can track everything we do that affects what we are unhappy about. If it's about health, track food intake, sleep, and physical activity. If it's about finances, track all incomes and all expenditures. If it's about work, maybe start a diary where we write down how we feel every day and what made us feel that way.

Tracking will give us the info we need. It reveals the truth about what we do and might even start our change while tracking. When we pay more attention, it will also influence our choices. We might even begin slowly changing what we do every day because keeping tabs makes every choice more conscious.

We can take a closer look when we have been tracking for a couple of weeks or months. What do we actually do? How much do we exercise? How much are we spending? How do we really feel about work? And what do the long-term consequences of that behavior look like?

Let's just take an example: Say we get a $5 Caramel Macchiato (Grande, 2 % fat milk) at Starbucks daily. That's $150 a month. Quite some money for coffee. It's also about 250 calories for each drink, or 7.500 calories a month. If we consider the money from more perspective, it's $1800 a year, or $9.000 in 5 years.

Wait a minute! Some $9.000 for caramel macchiato!? That's crazy! Imagine what we could do with that money. And those $9.000 are in today's money value. If we put that same money in the bank instead, compounded over time, it would turn out to be much more. Skip the lattes and retire rich!

And what about the calories? If we convert the calories to kilos, the 7.500 calories are just about one kilo of more fat on the body, everything else equal. That's in one month, adding 12 kilos extra in a year. Or adding 60 kilos in five years! Hello, obesity!

What do you say about this advertising headline: "Pay $9.000 to gain 60 kilos of fat in five years." How does that sound? Would it sell?

Here is an alternative use for that money: Spend a couple of weeks on a tropical island every second year, and we will still have money left to pay for a gym membership. Sounds more tempting than 60 kilos of fat, or?

Or we could just put the money to work by investing it. Don't forget that we would still save ourselves from 60 kilos of added fat in five years.

Tracking makes us pay attention to what we are actually doing. Questions to ask ourselves could be how it compares to what we thought we were doing? What results are our current actions producing? Once we know this, we will also see what needs to change. We can pinpoint what's creating the biggest problems for us. And then we can start to make changes.

If we once again focus on our purpose—what would you like to do, and when?

> *"If you don't know where you're going,*
> *any road will take you there."*
> ~ Lewis Carroll ~

When we know where we are and want to go, it's easier to make the everyday decisions that take us in that direction. To get different results, we need to change some things. Maybe even become a new person.

Why? Because the costs of *not* taking action are too high.

If you are unhappy now and don't change anything, what makes you think you will become happier in the future?

The costs of not acting also include the regrets we get knowing we *could* have made that change. And it will probably be more challenging to make the change later since we will be even further down that road.

Become the kind of person who gets the results you want.

Deserve it, and you will get it.

*"The best way to get what you want
is to deserve what you want."*
~ Charles Munger ~

Purpose

If what we want to change is related to health, weight, finances, or something very concrete, then it's not that difficult to figure out in which direction we must change. But we must think if we are unclear about what's wrong. If it's about how we make a living, we need to figure out what we really want—what do we want to achieve? What's our purpose? We have to use our imagination and dare to dream big.

*"Imagination should be used, not to escape
reality, but to create it."*
~ Colin Wilson ~

Sometimes discovering what we want is more complicated than making it come true. Remember that and dare to dream.

I believe that for many, this is something that can and will change over time.

I believe this is true for me. So, we don't need to look for something we will keep for the rest of our lives. We just have to make sure it's something that we enjoy a lot right now.

I know what I enjoy doing. I know I like to help people, whether it's to become better dancers or if it's improving their lives in other ways.

Here are some questions that can help you find direction:

- What gives you meaning?
- What do you want to achieve?
- What impact do you want to have on others?
- What do you want to do that positively affects their lives?
- In what way can you make the world a better place?
- What would make you feel that you matter?

What would you do if money wasn't an issue—if you didn't need to make money? What would fire you up? What would you do if it didn't matter what other people were thinking? What would you do if you knew you would succeed for sure? Or what would be worth doing even if you failed?

> *"What's money? A man is a success if he gets up in the morning and goes to bed at night and in between does what he wants to do."*
> ~ Bob Dylan ~

I believe too many people live lives they are not satisfied with. They don't follow their passions. They don't do something that makes them feel alive.

What's the problem with this? Well, first, they will not enjoy life as much. Work is a big part of life, and if we are not enjoying what we do, it means a big part of life is wasted. Second, it means that someone else will come along—someone who loves that job—and they will outwork the people who don't love it. They will work much more because they love what they do. When we love what we do, any problem at work is easy. If we don't love it, everything is a struggle. Everything feels meaningless when we don't enjoy what we do, and if that continues for too long, we might not have a job anymore.

Look for work that feels like play.

For some people, it's straightforward. They know what they want to do. Maybe they dreamt about it since they were five years old.

Dreaming about it for a long time doesn't necessarily mean that they already do it for a living, but at least they know.

Then we have the people who didn't know what they wanted to do when they started their studies or even finished them. I believe many people choose what to study not because of their interests but because of what society considers right or good. And finally, we have people who still don't know their purpose long after finishing their studies. If you are like that, here are some more questions to help you figure it out:

- What do you like to do in your spare time?
- Where does your mind wander when you have time off?
- What did you enjoy doing as a child before the rest of the world told you what you *should* do?
- What type of content do you like watching online? What topics?
- What do you like talking about?

Answering these questions can give some clues. What we enjoy doing in life leads us in the right direction. We just have to be sure it's something we will enjoy for a long time. Otherwise, it might just be a distraction.

Once we know what we enjoy, everything else, all that awaits us on the way, will be much easier.

Dig deep. Ask yourself "why" many times to find out what drives you. When you know what drives you, it will be much easier to keep going when you face some obstacles—because you love what you do.

Maybe you discover that you have several callings in life—several things you want to do—and different things over time. I know this is true for me. I have many things I want to do.

There's no need to just pick one and stick with it forever. Remember, almost no choices are permanent or irreversible. We change, and so can our choices.

"Don't let the noise of others' opinions drown out your own inner voice. And most important, have the courage to follow your heart and intuition. They somehow already know what you truly want to become."
~ Steve Jobs ~

If we don't do something we enjoy—something that gives us meaning—we will not find peace. Everything will feel like a struggle. When we don't have peace, we can't feel happy. Yes, we can find joy. We can have joyful moments, and that's great, but it's not true happiness.

We need to do something that ignites the fire inside and makes us feel alive. Because happiness is when we don't desire anything else. If we are not satisfied at work, we will have that desire for something else. And as long as we have that, we will not be happy.

There's actually a mental state that tells us we are on the right way. It's called "flow," and I am sure you have experienced it.

When we are balancing just on the edge of our capacity, we can experience it. It's the feeling we get when we focus on some activity and get totally absorbed by it. We hardly notice people talking to us. Nothing can distract us. We lose track of time. And suddenly, we realize it's three in the morning, and we should have eaten dinner a long time ago, but we didn't feel the hunger. And we know we will hardly sleep before getting up and returning to our daily routines. That's the experience of flow.

The psychologist Mihaly Csikszentmihalyi is the man who gave this feeling its name. He described this state as "pleasure, delight, creativity" when we are totally "immersed in life." To increase our chances of entering a state of flow, we should:

- Find something challenging to do but something we can handle. It can't be too easy, so we get bored, but also not too difficult, so we get frustrated. Best is something that's challenging and makes us just slightly uncomfortable.
- Have a clear objective—a clear goal. We need to know what we want to achieve with the activity. We should think of the objective but not obsess over it or stress out if we don't succeed immediately. We are not always on target, but if it's the right difficulty level, we will be able to do it.
- Focus. There are a million distractions and a million things we can do at any point in time. Some people believe in multi-tasking, but it's impossible to do two or more things simultaneously without lowering the quality of our work. And the chances of achieving flow decrease significantly when we try to multi-task.

So, we should focus on doing one thing at a time and limit distractions like phones and other things that call our attention.

If you want to get better at finding flow, you can try meditation. It can be as simple as sitting in a relaxed position for ten minutes, focusing on your breathing. Any thoughts that come into your mind, let them come, and then release them again to free your mind.

The more often we enter flow, the easier it will become. The more activities we do that let us enter flow, the more time we will spend in this state. And the more time we spend in flow, the happier we will be. So, when we find activities that let us enter flow, it's a clue, something worth listening to.

Imagine how your days at work would be if you do something you really enjoy and you enter flow daily. Your days at work will fly by, losing track of time. It will not feel like work. And you will get immense satisfaction from it. Search for those optimal experiences.

So, what do you really want to do in life? Or what change would make the absolute biggest difference in your life? If you try to be specific, what is it? Describe it in detail. What would it look like? Create a clear goal. How would you do it?

If we exemplify with losing weight, then "losing some weight" is not a good goal. Because once we have lost one or two kilos, we have essentially achieved it. "Some weight" is not specific enough. It's not quantified. And there's no time frame. So, we should try to set a clear, measurable, realistic, and relevant goal and give it a time frame. And the next step is to try to chunk it into pieces with shorter-term goals, write it down and place it somewhere visible. And then follow up.

What gets measured gets done. And improved.

Reaching self-actualization is not about dreaming or talking about doing something. It's about actually doing it. So, it's not enough to know what we want. We need to start, and we need to fight for it a lot, maybe every day. It will require sacrifices. But it will be worth it.

We often feel good when doing things we are good at. It gives us satisfaction. But we don't love all things we are good at. Being good or great at something doesn't necessarily mean we should continue doing it. It doesn't mean it's our purpose in life. We must ask ourselves if we want it before choosing to do it.

The people who genuinely fulfill their purpose love to wake up every morning. They have understood that life is not about waiting; for a promotion, the next job, or something else.

Life is now. The only moment you can control is now. And the only step that you need to pay attention to is the step you take now. There really is no other step you can take. Make it a good one!

So, try to make your choices in life out of love. Because this might be your only chance, your only life. You can choose to live at 50 % or 20 %. Or you can choose to live at 100 %. How will you spend the day? Doing something you hate? Or doing something you love—something that's entirely you. Remember, no one can compete with you on being you.

"Every man dies, not every man really lives."
~ William Wallace in "Braveheart" ~

When you are born, you have a blank slate in front of you. Nothing has been written yet. You write the story of your life. Nothing you do can change the story that was already written. But you get a chance to change the rest of that story every day. What will you write?

Ikigai

Something else which can help us find purpose is the concept of Ikigai. It's a Japanese word, and it's about living happy, healthy, and long lives. The term can loosely be translated as "happiness of always being busy." And there's something to it. Being busy can mean that we are needed. And when we feel needed, we feel we make a difference.

Everyone has a reason for being. But not all of us have found it. I think that, to a large extent, this is because we are forced onto specific paths in life, often because of what we feel are other people's expectations.

Why do you really get up in the morning? If you feel you get up effortlessly and feel happy about a new day, maybe you have found your ikigai because you look forward to what you will do. On the other hand, if you struggle and would rather stay in bed and not go to work, maybe you haven't found it yet.

Ikigai is a pretty broad concept, but in terms of purpose, you could say that it's in the intersection of these four:

- What you are good at
- What you love doing
- What you can make money from
- What the world needs

If we can find something that fulfills all those, we have found our Ikigai. We will find meaning in life. Then we will feel satisfaction and happiness. That in itself will contribute to a longer and healthier life.

As mentioned previously, I believe that:

If you love something, you will do it a lot. If you do it a lot, you will become good. And when you are good, you can make money.

So, with that, three of the four conditions for ikigai will be there over time. And it all starts with love. Something that we love doing.

The last part, what the world needs, is the missing link. But on the other hand, this is also very much up to our interpretation. We all have our different views on what the world needs.

> *"Don't ask what the world needs. Ask what makes*
> *you come alive, and go do it. Because what the*
> *world needs is people who have come alive."*
> ~ Howard Thurman ~

It's really down to finding something we love doing that would make the world a better place in some way. And then it's just hard work. But it's fun work. Something that will not feel like work. I know it can take a lot of courage to go for what we love. We might feel terrified. I know I did. But if we accept that feeling and try to take charge of our actions every day, we will move towards that goal, doing what we love today.

Zigzagging Forward

Once we know what we want to do, everything becomes clear. Even if we don't know precisely what steps to take or in what order, we will know in which direction we need to move. We just have to keep going that way.

If we have done something before, we will know the exact steps to take to get there. We might not know the fastest or best way, but we know that if we take those steps, we will get there.

When we do something for the first time, we know neither what to do nor in what order to do it. So, we need to try something that makes sense and seems reasonable. And then we pay attention. We check the results and must accept that we will sometimes make mistakes. We might end up at dead ends. And any time we notice we get off track, we can try to correct it and get back on track. With every step we take, we can learn something—also from our mistakes. Or maybe even more from the mistakes.

"I have not failed. I've just found 10,000 ways that won't work."
~ Thomas A. Edison ~

If we are not making any mistakes, we might not be on the right path because we are not challenging ourselves. We are not reaching for our highest potential. We are taking the easy way out. Dare to challenge yourself. And don't be afraid.

If you are off track, just compensate the zig with a bit of zag.

Airplanes on autopilot are only on the right course for a small part of the trip. Most of the time, they are off course. But they are constantly correcting it. This is true for most endeavors in life too. Don't get discouraged by being off course. If the general direction is correct, you are doing the right thing. Just correct the course slightly.

When we realize that we can only fail if we don't try and accept that we will be off course most of the time, it will be much easier to give it a try. It will be easier to conquer our fears and go for it.

"Our greatest weakness lies in giving up. The most certain way to succeed is always to try just one more time."
~ Thomas A. Edison ~

How do we know we are off course? First, we must listen to our bodies. If we feel uneasy about something, it tells us we are not doing the right thing. If we must do things that don't align with our values, then we are not doing the right thing. Another clue *can* be if we are not yet getting the results we are after. I italicize "can" because it's just a possibility. It can also be that we didn't try enough. But if we have already tried for a long time, we can be on the wrong track. Maybe it's not for us. But if we decide to quit, we must make sure we are quitting for the right reasons. Not getting quick results is expected. It can also mean we need to stay at it a bit longer for results to come. It can be hard to tell which one it is, so we must listen to our feelings.

Sometimes being off track can also be a good thing. We might discover a new path. The unexpected might happen. Sometimes what we least expect could be the right thing for us. So, pay attention!

Going with the Flow

Our imagination may be amazing. Our goals in life could be too. And still, life could be even more amazing. It could have other things in store for us—something that really surprises us.

We have talked a lot about finding some kind of purpose in life. I think it makes sense to try to find it—and then try to live by it. It gives us a direction in life. If you really want something, I think you should go after it with determination. That's what a big part of this book is about.

But I also believe that sometimes we should just go with the flow. Life is unpredictable. It can take us to places we never expected. Opportunities that we never thought were possible can arise. And we can become something that we never dreamt of. Even something we never thought we would enjoy.

If we don't reach our original goal, we can still end up somewhere we feel perfectly happy. A different place, but still great, or maybe even better than our original plan. In a way, life can save us from something we think we want and give us something we need. A little gift from life itself.

I am an example of this. I have a business degree. I worked with marketing online and became a bit of an expert in viral marketing. I am analytical and naturally a thinker. At work, I often preferred doing my thinking alone and sometimes didn't enjoy client meetings that much. I was never socially incompetent, but a bit introverted and not fond of talking in front of a crowd or on a stage. More correctly, I hated it. It terrified me.

Around 2000 I started social dancing. First Salsa, and then Bachata. I really loved it, and I had social dancing as a hobby during my spare time. I used to dance several times weekly, doing it just for fun. And my social dancing got the attention of dance schools. They asked me to get on their student teams for Salsa and Bachata. I always said no because I didn't want to perform. Even as an adult, it was still very uncomfortable for me to be standing on a stage. And much more so to talk or dance.

But around 2010, I began to conquer this fear. I started to get requests from companies as an expert in viral marketing. I was asked to do a couple of guest lectures at business schools in

Stockholm. After some hesitation, I accepted, and even if I was very nervous before the talks, I kind of liked the feeling of sharing my knowledge and helping the students learn.

Then in 2011, I found Kizomba. You already read about it in the introduction.

I started going to festivals around Europe, and as one of the first who began dancing Kizomba in Sweden, I got asked to start teaching others. Initially, I thought it was just to substitute the original teacher for four classes. But it turned out it was a misunderstanding, and I realized the school wanted me to give the whole course. After some thinking and some discussions, I said yes. It was undoubtedly a challenge, and I didn't feel comfortable initially. But I liked teaching, and apparently, my students liked my classes too. So, word spread, and I started getting requests for workshops in other cities in Sweden and countries around Europe.

The more I taught, the more comfortable I felt. I started getting used to it, and over time I got more and more requests from all over the world. But traveling to teach on weekends while still working full time was tough. I was tired, working during the week with marketing and traveling all over Europe almost every weekend. Late nights on weekends made me sleep too little, and I got increasingly worn out. Keeping everything on track started to become a challenge.

So, I had to decide. I decided to quit my day job and take this once-in-a-lifetime opportunity. Soon I was traveling all over the world.

A Master of Science in Business Administration who turned into an international dance teacher. When writing this, I have been teaching in more than 60 countries and 150 cities. All because I decided to go with the flow.

I decided to conquer my fears of talking in front of people and my concerns about not having a fixed income. And to be honest, I am much happier now than sitting in an office for 40+ hours per week.

I believe in following the dreams we have. But I think we should also listen to life—listen to the little hints we get. If we pay attention and take the unexpected opportunities that appear in front of us, life can take us to places we never thought were possible.

I already knew I loved dancing. That was never the issue. It was more about accepting and conquering my fear of talking in front of people and realizing that making a good living as a dance teacher was possible.

*"Two roads diverged in a wood and I—I took the one
less traveled by, and that has made all the difference."*
Robert Frost

We should dare to take the road less traveled. And accept that what "less traveled" means is different for everyone.

It can seem like a step in the wrong direction. Something that takes us off course and needs to be corrected. But if we pay attention—if we stop and feel—we might discover it was just right. If we have the courage, we might find something we never expected.

*"Life has more imagination than
we carry in our dreams."*
~ Christopher Columbus ~

Your current plan is just a decision you made at some point. Whenever you want, you can change course. Don't be afraid to go with the flow sometimes. What seems like a disaster might turn out to be a blessing. It could change your life forever.

HOW THE WORLD WORKS

Entitlement

It's time to talk seriously. This might be heavy to take. So, sit down and relax. Take a deep breath. Here we go.

You deserve better. You do. But only if you make an effort. Entitlement is a problem for many people. You might think that you deserve more. You might sometimes feel it's not worth it to make an effort because you will not get what you deserve anyway. But in the long run, the world doesn't work like that. In general, we get what we deserve. So, when we think we deserve more than we get, it's time to make a reality check.

Maybe we aren't as good as we think? Perhaps we aren't better than what *others* think we are? Maybe *others* are better at judging our performance than *we* are. And maybe our efforts don't deserve more than the results indicate.

There's a psychological phenomenon called the above-average effect or superiority bias. We often think that we are better than we are. When researching for this book, I found that around 90 % of people consider themselves above average in any specific skill. Anyone understanding averages can see that 90 % cannot be better than average. Only 50 % can be. Even more interesting about this superiority effect is that the worse the actual performance, the stronger the effect.

We must remember we are only the center of the universe to ourselves. No one is as interested in what we do as we are, and maybe our mom.

In general, effort gets a fair payoff. Whether it's an effort in the professional sphere, about losing weight, or something else. If the results are not what we think we deserve, the best thing we can do is face reality and try a bit harder. Do more.

If you think the world is somehow against you, it's not true. The world is not against you. Others are not out to get you. No one cares enough about you to try to make you fail. They are too busy with their own lives. They have enough of their own struggles and problems, managing their own lives.

The world is not against anyone. It's against everyone in a way. If you just do average, you will not succeed. If you don't make an effort, the world will not reward you more than anyone else. But when you do a little bit more than everybody else, the world starts paying attention. And the more you do, the more attention you get. Opportunities turn up, and things start going your way.

"As a man changes his own nature, so does the
attitude of the world change towards him."
~ Mahatma Gandhi ~

Mindset

Do you believe in destiny? I do. And I don't.

There are two meanings of the word "destiny." One is basically "the things that will happen in the future." The other is "the force that some people think controls what happens in the future and is outside human control." So, do you believe in destiny? I do. And I don't. In the word's first meaning, we would have to believe as long as we think there will be a future. In the second meaning of the word, I don't believe it. I don't believe there's some kind of force that controls what will happen, over which I have no control. I believe we can shape our future—or "destiny," if you like. As you might already have noticed, I like quotes, and here is one that I really like:

"The only person you are destined to become
is the person you decide to be."
~ Ralph Waldo Emerson ~

Actually, I don't like it. I love it! Because it means we have the power. There's no uncontrollable "destiny." We decide and control what happens in our lives. We determine who we become. It's incredibly empowering. And this quote is probably my all-time favorite:

> *"Whether you think that you can or think*
> *that you can't, you're right!"*
> ~ Henry Ford ~

It shows how our own mindset and beliefs control reality and the future. If we truly believe, we can do it! If we don't, we can't.

It turns out that these are not just some old, dusty life quotes from significant historical figures. It turns out research has shown them to be true. It has been proven that we are not predetermined or "fixed." We can change and grow, and the master switch—the most important factor—for whether we succeed or not is our beliefs.

- If we have the beliefs that we *can* change—that we *can* get better.
- Or whether we believe we already *are* in a certain way and *cannot* change that.

It makes sense. If we believe we cannot change, we will not change because it's not even worth trying when we don't think we can. But if we believe we can, we will hopefully give it a try, and that's the only way we can give ourselves a chance to change. *Trying* makes it possible. *Not* trying is the surest way to ensure we will not change.

"The only failure is not trying."
~ Robin S. Sharma ~

But why do we end up with one belief or the other? A lot has to do with how we have been raised. Kids have a growth mindset by nature. They try, they explore, and they experiment. They don't seem to feel fear. They want to grow. They are constantly on the edge of their capabilities. They learn how to crawl, then how to walk, and then how to run. They take a step, and they fall, over and over. But they always get back up. They are full of life and curiosity.

Their parents and other adults encourage them. Parents also praise them. But praise can be about different things. The praise we are exposed to as a child has a tremendous effect on how we think later. For example, suppose we are constantly praised for our results and told we are intelligent or talented. In that case, we often think we are just that. What's being praised is our talent or intelligence. This is what we are or what we have. We learn that there are intelligent and dumb people—talented and untalented. This can lead to a "fixed mindset."

Basically, it's telling us we were born in a certain way, and that's how we are—we cannot change it. So, we believe that if we fail, it's because we are not really that intelligent or not that talented. And we might think that if we succeeded before, maybe it was just some stroke of luck?

For these people, failure at something means just failure. So, it makes sense that people with this mindset gradually start avoiding difficult tasks more and more. Because then they minimize the risk of failure. They don't want to risk looking "stupid" or feeling like a failure. The brain is telling them: "Don't do it. Don't take the risk." So, they stay within their comfort zone where they feel sure they will succeed. They do nothing that might result in "failure." They stop challenging themselves. They stop being curious. They stop developing. The only thing they might still do is dream. But they don't try. They don't do anything. And that's where it all ends. Sure, they can't fail, but there's also no chance of success if they don't even try.

Luckily there's another type of praise that creates another mindset. When praise is directed toward the effort and learning experience, kids learn that they are worthy of praise when they try. *Trying* is good. *They* are good as long as they try, regardless of the result. The focus is on the effort, and they learn that they can grow their intelligence, skill, and even their personality when they keep trying.

This is the "growth mindset." Kids learn to see failure as "learning," and learning is good. Kids who know how to think like this don't avoid failure. They keep trying and keep putting in the effort. And the brain tells them: Go for it! Give it a try! If you fall, just get up! If you work on it, you will get better. And then you will succeed. You can make it happen.

The battle between "nature or nurture"—whether we depend more on our genes or the environment—is still not settled. Most people believe we rely on both. But recently, we have learned that the effect of nurture is much more significant than we ever thought. And the "growth mindset" is needed if we want to keep growing.

People who have this mindset keep pushing themselves. They love a challenge, even if they might fail at first. They know that they will learn and grow from it. On the other hand, people with a fixed mindset avoid any challenge that they are not sure they will be able to handle. But then, it's no longer a challenge, and they will not grow or learn from it.

If we have a fixed or a growth mindset is not an either-or question. Most people lie along a scale between them. And they can be on opposite sides of the scale in different areas of life.

Believing our capabilities are fixed or that we can change and grow makes a huge difference over a lifetime. Thinking that effort is a waste of time or that it pays off; that we are intelligent or not; talented or not. All those small decisions we make in life as a result of these beliefs add up. Not putting in more effort because if we put in the effort and still fail, it must mean we are stupid or untalented. Or not taking a challenge because we might fail, which means we are not good enough. All these moments of avoiding possibilities where we could have stretched ourselves and learned add up and multiply. In the end, the number of opportunities lost, the lessons not understood, and the chances not taken will limit our lives tremendously.

You don't know your limit. Thinking you are a certain way will limit you. Just believing you have a limit will limit you.

People with a fixed mindset often dream of being on top, just a little better than everybody else. Just a little bit more admired than everybody else. Ironically, they rarely get there because they fear the risk of failure so much they don't even put in the effort. They fear the challenges they need to accept to get there. They don't dare to take chances to get there. They might never even get those chances. Because someone who values effort and does everything they can to learn and develop will get those chances instead.

Now, here comes the good news—we can change our mindset. It's possible to get more of a growth mindset, and if we change our mindset, it has a lot of positive effects.

We don't need to fear failure. We can constantly think we are here to learn. We are here to grow. As long as we give it a try, it's great. Success will teach us, but we might learn even more from failure. So, there's nothing to fear.

"Failure is the key to success; each mistake teaches us something."
~ Morihei Ueshiba ~

When we stop believing that we either have talent or put in the effort, we will also realize that we can combine them, and they are much more powerful. Talent plus effort. Just because we are aware of the different mindsets means we can start changing ours.

To do that, we must pay attention. First, we need to figure out our current mindset. We must be aware of our actions and why we do what we do. If we choose not to do something, why is that? If we don't take a challenge, why is that? Then we will know if those decisions come from a growth or a fixed mindset. And then we can start doing something about it.

Since most mindsets are not pure growth or fixed, changing mindsets is the same—it's not a one-time event and a 100 % change that lasts forever. It's more like one of them is the dominant one. And, like so many other things in life, it's a process. Sometimes the old thinking and the old fears might come back. Sometimes the new thinking is stronger.

It's essential to constantly try to cultivate the new growth mindset and strengthen it. Eventually, it will be the dominant one, affecting our thoughts, feelings, and actions for the rest of our lives. So, what can we do?

- When things get tough, and you feel like quitting because you don't think you will make it. Keep going! The longer you keep at it, the longer you learn. You will practice both your willpower and your new mindset.

- Search for people who don't just praise you but rather give you constructive criticism—people who offer something you can learn from. Have you "failed" at something? Now try to look at it from another angle. What exactly did you do? What can you learn from it? What can you do better next time? Remember that effort is not bad. An effort is needed every time you challenge your limits. If there's no effort, you are not learning anything new, and you want to learn. You want to grow.

- Whenever you get an opportunity to do something you would like, take it. At a minimum, you could learn something. Even if it might be beyond your capabilities or what you *think* are your capabilities. If you stretch yourself, you can make it. And if you don't make it, it was still worth it. Remember: The only failure is not trying.

- Our mindset is fundamental for everything we do in life. So, we should keep a growth mindset and help our kids develop one.

"You miss 100 % of the shots you don't take."
~ Wayne Gretzky ~

If you want to read more about mindset and get other book recommendations, check the further reading pages at: unsucklife.net/further-reading

Action vs. Inaction

People have sometimes asked me how I have time to do so much. I seem quite active, but if I compare the number of ideas I have realized with the number of ideas I have, my output is quite low. I always try to learn things, and then my mind gives me new ideas. I have a creative mind, and I am most definitely a thinker. But I was not a real doer until I started writing this book. I have felt that I need to do more for a long time. Not think, do. And it's beginning to change.

> *"Ideas are worthless until you do*
> *something with them."*
> ~ Mark Cuban ~

I admit I have been a procrastinator. I always started late on school projects and finished just before the deadline. I usually started studying the last days before an exam. When trying to catch a flight or a train, I am always on time, but I frequently arrive just in time or maybe a few minutes late if it isn't a fixed deadline. Perhaps you recognize these behaviors?

For a procrastinator, things somehow still work out when there's a deadline. At least if they suffer from one of the milder versions of procrastination. Because they panic in the end and work like crazy. Somehow, they survive the stress and manage to deliver. The quality isn't as good as it could have been, but they make it.

However, there are circumstances when procrastination is much worse. There are cases when it has a much more devastating effect. Like when there's no deadline. Because then they never panic. They can go on forever procrastinating, never getting to that point of panic when they actually start doing something.

We already know it: "Ideas are worthless until you do something with them." And when it comes to our dreams and ideas, we are incredibly vulnerable to procrastination since no one has put a deadline on them. Unless we do it ourselves.

In most cases, intentions do not matter. Actions do, and action always beats inaction. First, we decide, and then we act. Not making a decision is also a kind of decision over time—not to do anything.

‣ Stop thinking.
‣ Stop talking.
‣ Start doing

If we don't start, we don't change anything. Avoiding the start is what procrastinators are world champions at. But what, besides the obvious, are some signs to look out for?

- Being indecisive is a sign of procrastination. You are afraid of making mistakes, so you postpone and avoid important decisions.
- Being unclear about goals is another sign. If the goal is not defined, there's nothing to work for yet, so you don't need to start.
- Being unrealistic about time is yet another. You are often late. You miss deadlines. You don't really know how you spend your time. It just seems to fly by. You lose opportunities, not because of "you" but because you "ran out of time." You protect your ego this way. It wasn't your fault, just not enough time.

We need to be clear about what we want to do. We need to have a vision. But it's not enough.

> *"Vision is not enough.*
> *It must be combined with venture.*
> *It's not enough to stare up the steps.*
> *We must step up the stairs."*
> ~ Václav Havel ~

We often procrastinate because we have learned to fear failure. We want to avoid the risk of criticism. But strangely enough, it can also be that we fear success. If we succeed, it might mean we have to change many things. The status quo often feels safe.

Procrastination can be a tool to handle our anxiety—the anxiety we can get from starting or finishing something.

When there are too many things we procrastinate on, we start living life at half speed. Nothing is as fast as it could be, and life slows down. Not much gets done.

If you struggle with procrastination, remember you are not only a procrastinator. When you need to do something you enjoy, you don't procrastinate, do you? So, it's not who you are. It's the situation. It's the task you avoid.

If we tend to procrastinate, we need to be clearer about our goals and take action. If we do *something*, it's always better than doing *nothing*. We can all agree on that. It just makes sense. Even if this something seems pretty tiny and ridiculous. But doing something, even negligible, builds up to quite a lot over time. It's also often better to do something small many times than trying to do a lot only once. It's better for your body to run three kilometers every second day than trying to run a marathon once a month. Even if the total distance is about the same.

> *"Even if you are on the right track, you will get run over if you just sit there."*
> ~ Will Rogers ~

Starting breaks the status quo. Things start changing. The momentum we build when we do something every day is also a big help. And the longer we keep at it, the easier it gets.

Another benefit is that action produces information. We learn. Before we act, we cannot know. We just have theories. Once we start, we get the real world feedback.

In addition, the effect on our self-esteem is possibly worth even more. We become doers. We practice winning. Over time we build a pattern of finishing, and our identity starts shifting.

Once you start, you become a doer, and when you are a doer, you are more likely to finish. The more you finish, the more you expect to finish, and the easier it will be to start next time because you know you are the kind of person who finishes.

We need to take the first step. Inertia keeps an object still unless some force pushes it in some direction. Once it's in motion, that same inertia keeps it in motion unless something stops it. This same law works for us too. We need to take the first step and get started.

> *"You can't build a reputation on what you are going to do."*
> ~ Henry Ford ~

Once we are in motion, everything is easier, and momentum works *for* us. One step today, one step tomorrow, one step the day after. Keep pushing in the right direction. Keep putting one foot in front of the other towards the goal.

And on the flip side of starting more, we also have to avoid quitting. Every time we quit, we make it a little bit easier to quit the next time. And the longer we quit, the more momentum is lost.

> *"Action is the foundational key to all success."*
> ~ Pablo Picasso ~

Only one thing guarantees we will never reach our dreams—not taking that first step. Just like time, inertia works *for* us or *against* us. As long as we don't try to get out of that sofa, we will stay on that sofa. If we don't start the change and get that momentum going, we will forever regret not taking the first step. The reason most people don't live their dreams is precisely this. They never take the first step.

Perfectionism

Perfectionism overlaps a lot with procrastination and exhibits similar traits. But while the procrastinator often finds it difficult to start, the perfectionist starts but doesn't finish. In the end, the results are comparable.

I have sometimes suffered from it. "Suffer," you might wonder. Yes, I have come to believe that perfectionism is bad for us in many ways, and makes us suffer. It has affected many projects in my life, not in a good way. And I am not the only one who's afflicted. I believe it's quite common. Maybe you suffer from it too?

There are many problems with perfectionism. First, anyone with this affliction knows we will spend too much time on everything we do. We will worry about imagined and potential issues, trying to find solutions for them. In addition, we will also spend way too much time on the wrong things—the things that don't matter.

I am starting to think that perfectionism is rooted in some insecurity—that we want it to be impossible to criticize or improve on what we do. But, of course, creating something perfect is impossible to achieve. And therefore, perfectionism has a real downside.

Searching for perfection will make us unhappy because it's a search that has no end. It's impossible to find.

And this also has significant consequences for our productivity:

> *"The perfect is the enemy of the good"*
> ~ Voltaire ~

When we try to make something perfect, we often don't make anything at all because we never finish. We never deliver.

I know it's easy to justify to ourselves why we want it to be perfect. Why *wouldn't* we want it perfect? It would be the best it can be. I admit I struggled with the idea, but I have realized that the search for perfection is fruitless at best, and likely counterproductive.

An idea is useless until we do something with it, and it cannot have much value until we deliver it into this world. So, we need to deliver.

To deliver we need momentum, and when we strive for perfection, momentum dies out. In the end, searching for perfection often leads to nothing. It's constantly a "work in progress," and that's why we never finish.

"Perfect" doesn't exist. The truth is that you will have a better idea. And every day, you will get better, so tomorrow you will be able to produce something even better. Don't wait for perfection. If you do, you will wait forever.

So how can we battle the search for perfection? Well, there are some things we can do to fight it, and some are the same as how we fight procrastination:

‣ Give it a deadline. Nothing promotes perfectionism more than when we don't have a deadline. Then we can think about and work on it forever. And the second worst is a deadline that we can move. When we start postponing, we can extend the deadline into eternity. Instead, we must use deadlines as our weapon, prioritizing progress over perfection.

‣ Give it a new endpoint. We must realize that there is a point where we have to stop—where it's good enough. Very often, the 80/20-rule applies: we can achieve about 80 % of the output in just 20 % of the time, so it is better not to spend the other 80 % of the time trying to achieve the last 20 %. I know "good enough" is not a great endpoint. I mean, when is it good enough? It's not something objective but very subjective. Still, it's better than "perfect." And I am sure you understand the idea I want to convey.

‣ We must also clarify the alternative costs of what we do and prioritize. It is better to "satisfice"—make something good enough and then move on to what's next. It will be easier to know what needs to be improved when we get feedback from the world. In the meantime, we have started working on the next step. We keep momentum, and once we get feedback, we improve on it.

‣ Finally, we must accept that the search for perfection is futile. It will never be perfect, and we will make mistakes. It's part of the process. Accept it and keep moving.

Remember that happiness is when we don't desire something else or something more. So, striving for perfection, that doesn't even exist, will make us unhappy.

Responsibility

There's a massive difference between blaming external factors and taking own responsibility. When we blame external factors, we give away our control. When we take 100 % responsibility, we also get 100 % power to change things.

We are responsible for getting a job, making enough money to survive, saving for retirement, etc. But this is not enough to say we are taking full responsibility. We are also responsible for our relations with others and how we respond to what's happening in life. We are responsible for our own happiness.

As long as we keep complaining about what happens in life, what others do or say, or how we feel about it, we are not taking responsibility. Yes, maybe for what we do, but not for how we feel or react to things.

If someone makes you feel bad—why don't you tell them? Why are you still friends? Why do you let them? Or if you didn't get that promotion—why did someone else get it instead of you? Did you really do all you could do to get it? Was there anything more you could have done to get it? If you still smoke from time to time—could you do something more to avoid the temptation? There's always something to learn. There's always something more we can do. It's always within our control.

Complaining doesn't help. If we complain and blame others or external factors, we act like victims. And if we consider ourselves a victim, we are powerless. Of course, being a victim can be pretty comfortable. We are safe inside your comfort zone. No need to do anything that requires that we step out of that zone. Just put the blame on others or external factors. Unfortunately, placing blame offers no way forward and no chance of progress. It's out of our hands.

So, we need to pay attention when this happens. When do we blame our situation on others or on external factors? If we ignore this, we will not know when we are not taking responsibility. We will not know when we need to change things.

Placing blame is just a destructive coping mechanism. When we don't take responsibility, we don't really need to learn or change anything. Because it was never our fault, right?

You understand where I am getting. Taking responsibility is the first step. By accepting responsibility, we also open up for learning. We realize we need to do something different next time to avoid that situation.

"I'm starting with the man in the mirror
I'm asking him to change his ways
And no message could've been any clearer
If you wanna make the world a better place
Take a look at yourself and then make a change."
~ Michael Jackson – "Man in the Mirror" ~

Responsibility also means knowing what we want and acting to make it happen. Many people just wait for things to happen in life—a promotion, finding the perfect partner, or some magical stroke of luck that will solve everything. And these people also tend to complain about their situation. Without action, we are not really taking responsibility.

To stop complaining is not enough. Action is required to really take responsibility for life.

We have all the power if we take responsibility and start taking action. We will not *wait* for it to happen but *make* it happen! We are in control.

Luck & Talent

When I am writing this, I am living a dream life. Yes, it's sometimes tiring, I must get up some very early mornings, and I often don't sleep enough. But I get to do something I love. I teach dance over the world. I get to travel, eat delicious food, and meet amazing people. Sometimes I go to places I never expected to visit, even in my wildest imagination. I have been teaching in more than 60 countries and 150 cities worldwide. When writing this sentence, I am in the Dominican Republic. It's warm and pleasant. But I have also been to Siberia five times, always in Winter. And I just got a booking for a small island in the Indian Ocean. Seeing this from the outside, who could complain about that kind of life?

However, what's not so visible from the outside is that there's a long story behind it. A tale of passion, hard work, dedication, sacrifices, persistence, a bit of coincidence, and a lot of courage.

"Overnight successes" are rarely overnight. "Blind luck," when something you have absolutely no control over happens, is very rare. There's almost always a long story behind the events we casually call an overnight success.

When we look at other people who succeed, we often believe they made it quickly. We think they are "talented" or "lucky." But talent rarely or ever takes you all the way. And luck—if you win the lottery, it's a decent example of blind luck. But the chances of winning are minimal. I don't recommend relying on the lottery to become rich.

Still, if we look closely at the lottery example, we can find something there that's key in life. Something we can learn from. No one wins the lottery if they don't buy a ticket. The ticket created a possibility. And creating possibilities is critical.

When we increase the number of possibilities in life, we have a bigger chance of success. We have to buy the ticket. We must do something. We have to try.

Someone working with their passion is not luck.

What we think is luck is usually just hard work for a long time. The hard work created the opportunity and made that person ready. And then they dared to take advantage of it when it came.

Luck

It happens that people tell me I am lucky, and I can imagine why it might seem so. For some reason, people want to believe in luck. They want to believe that things can change in a big way someday. I think it gives some kind of hope. But waiting is a bad idea.

Waiting for luck to strike only requires minimal effort, if even that. And nothing great ever comes from minimal effort.

When people tell me I'm lucky, I always start by saying: "No, it's not luck." This quote comes a bit closer to how things work in real life:

> *"I'm a great believer in luck and I find the*
> *harder I work, the more I have of it."*
> ~ Thomas Jefferson ~

Life really favors people who help themselves. It gives them "luck.". But there are two parts to what we often call "luck." Both require something from us. The first one is like a light switch—on or off. Either you have a chance, or you don't. As we said, it's like buying a lottery ticket or not buying it. If we don't buy it, there's no chance of winning.

We must expose ourselves to luck, or what people generally think is luck. If we want to win in sports but never participate in a competition, we have no chance of winning. We can't win if we don't even play. So, we need to take part. We must take advantage of the small windows of opportunity that life sends us. These can be bigger or smaller. What defines our destiny is how we respond to them. Do we take them or not? Do we shy away from them, or do we face the fear and jump on them? That's the first part—are we in or out?

The second part is a lot of work, and it's not on or off. It's on a scale, and the more, the better. We need to invest a lot of time and money in many cases. We must dedicate ourselves and make sacrifices. The more effort we put in, the more we increase our odds—we increase the "surface area of luck," so to speak.

Winners don't win because of luck. They win because they do the work. And then maybe, just maybe, they get a little bit of luck. Like if one runner gets disturbed by a flying insect and someone else wins the 100 meters Olympic final with two milliseconds. That win might be attributed to luck. But coming to the Olympics final wasn't luck. The winner didn't produce that time because of luck. It was hard work.

Besides all the work, we also need courage. Enough of it to go against what others expect from us. And enough to take the opportunities that present themselves to us once we have done our work. If we want something, we have to give it a try. We can't hesitate.

Work hard. Make sacrifices. Spend time and money if you need to. Only then will you have the chance to be there, at the right moment, ready for what's going to happen. And then you must have the courage to jump. This is what "luck" really is.

Be ready. The opportunity might come, but success rarely comes the first time we try. We will face setbacks. Maybe we will fail at first. We will sometimes crash and burn. But if we don't dare to jump, we will never fly. We can't wait for luck to come to us. We have to create our own luck. Remember, good things happen to people who do good things!

Talent

People also say I am talented quite often, and we hear people talk about talent all the time. Almost everything in life has indeed been quite easy for me so far. I "got" things fast in school, sports, and other parts of life. And especially when it comes to dancing, I can understand why they think so. It's what I do for a living, so I should be good.

But the one thing that has made it possible for me to be where I am today—to do what I do—is not luck or talent. It's dedication. It's persistence. It's consistency in what I do.

I have always been this way when I want to learn something. I do it for real. I go all in. You could say I become obsessed. I try to learn as much as possible and as fast as possible.

Of course, the fact that dedication is essential doesn't mean that what we call talent is unimportant. We are all born with specific talents. We have genes that give us a particular body and certain inclinations. If we want to be the best in the world in basketball, it helps if we are pretty tall. But being born with a talent doesn't mean you will get anything for free. It just makes it a bit easier to get it.

Talent is meaningless unless you do something with it. It's not what you have. It's what you do with what you have.

This is what it's like for everyone. Our genes do not decide whether we will succeed or not. They just make it easier in some areas and more difficult in others.

You can't just assume that people who succeed are more talented. Unless you have worked as hard as they have, you can't know who has more talent, can you?

In the long run, dedication is much more important than talent for most skills. If we have both, great! But if we don't have dedication, we will never become all we can be.

I hear people talking about "luck" and "talent" all the time. It's much rarer that people talk about or compliment the dedication and hard work that's always behind success.

This is because we fall for an illusion. We see what seems like an overnight success. Someone who appears out of nowhere. Someone we had never heard about before but suddenly seems to be everywhere. It appears to be talent, or maybe just luck. But we often don't see what came earlier—all the work.

In other cases, we realize there's a lot of work behind—like the big sports stars. They were very consistent and trained harder than we can imagine. They probably had talent, but we also know and understand that they have been training hard for a long time to become the best in the world. They had clear priorities. They made sacrifices. And they had a lot of dedication.

Often, we seem to forget about the commitment needed to become great at something. What we often call luck or talent is usually much more about motivation, willpower, and the ability to persist in the boredom that can come from repeating the same thing over and over.

Progress is not an event—it's a process. Consistent action leads to progress. And the key to consistent action is persistence.

The good news is that if we don't want to become the absolute best in the world at some sport, we don't need to become that obsessed. But we need to make an effort. We must be persistent and believe that what we do is the right thing to achieve the goal. Because we will not see significant results in the beginning. The changes will come only with time. Progress comes slowly. So, if we don't believe in it enough, we might quit too early.

The biggest problem I see with believing in "luck" and "talent" isn't that we ignore all the hard work and courage behind success. The biggest problem is that it prevents many people from living their dream.

When we believe we need to be lucky or talented to achieve our dreams and think we are neither, we might automatically exclude ourselves. It's not about luck or talent—it's about dedication.

You don't have a chance, if you don't give it a chance.

Pretty early in life, many people discover that they are not more talented than others, and they don't feel that luck is helping either, so they quit. Or they might never even start. But in reality, what we really need is neither luck nor talent but dedication, and that's something we can control. What does this mean for us?

Whether you consider yourself lucky or unlucky, whether you consider yourself talented or untalented, you can get whatever you want.

You need to put in a lot of work, you need to have some courage, and you need to take some chances to achieve your dreams. But you can do it!

Let's play a game: Imagine you are on the last day of your life, meeting the person you could have been? I mean the person you would be if you followed all your dreams and passions and achieved everything you wanted. What would it feel like? What would that person look like? How would that person behave? What would that person have done in life? What would their memories be like? How would they feel about the life they lived?

Now, if we return to the present—are you on a path to becoming that person? Is the life you are living right now supporting that dream life? Or are you heading in another direction? And where would that direction take you? Which life do you prefer? And most importantly—what do you need to start doing now to live that dream life in the end?

Remember, you are the one in charge. Show the world what you want! You just might get it!

Fear & Courage

Not too many thousand years ago, we needed fear. Wild animals and other tribes could threaten or even kill us. Unusual situations required some fear for us to be able to survive. The most fearless helped the rest of us survive, but they were probably also the most short-lived. We needed to pay attention, and we needed to react fast sometimes. And we needed to have some fear to do that.

In those days, fear meant standing face to face with a saber-toothed tiger, a cave bear, or an angry herd of mammoths.

Sometimes we needed to face the fear and attack the beast threatening us. We had to fight for our lives. And sometimes we had to give in to fear, avoid them and flee. But fear served a purpose. It helped us make good decisions. Sometimes we needed to feel fear, so we decided *not* to attack when we were alone. Otherwise, we might get injured and die. Maybe we didn't get any dinner that day, but at least we were alive.

Today we still fear many things, but it's a different kind of fear. It might be fear of a stock crash, that a date will be bad, or just the social consequences of saying or doing something that makes us look bad. It could be starting a relationship or ending one. Or it could be changing careers or not getting a promotion.

Sure, some of these things might sound terrifying. But no matter how terrifying, they are not about life and death.

Thousands of years ago, fear helped us stay alive. Nowadays, fear isn't as helpful. More than anything, it prevents us from doing what we really want.

Fear doesn't help us stay alive. It holds us back from living.

Yes, sometimes fear might help save our ego so that we seem to be the person we want to be. But sometimes, it doesn't even do that. Instead, it keeps us the way we think *others* want us to be.

Considering what people regret on their deathbeds, what we really should fear is not being true to ourselves.

So, we need to conquer the fear of not being liked. We need to stop thinking of what other people will think of us. We need to allow ourselves to be happy.

Fear is probably the biggest obstacle we face to becoming what we want to be. We fear not making enough money to pay the bills. We fear trying and failing. We might even fear success. And maybe more than anything, we fear other people's opinions. So, most people don't even try.

But fear is just that, an obstacle on the way. Courage is what we need to conquer that fear. We need to balance whatever we fear with enough courage to keep going.

> *"All our dreams can come true, if we have*
> *the courage to pursue them."*
> ~ Walt Disney ~

I would guess everybody feels fear from time to time. Yet, some people dare to face it. They look fear in the eye and don't look down. They feel it, ignore it, and go out and do whatever they want to do. From the outside, it seems like they don't feel fear at all, but I think they have just realized they can conquer it, so they do.

Others become totally paralyzed by fear. They prefer the status quo. And that can be perfectly fine *if* and *only* if they are happy where they are.

It can be fine for you too. If there's nothing in life you want to change, you don't need to challenge fear. But if there's something you wish was better, one little thing you would like to change, and the thought it frightens you, then you must face fear.

Remember, fear doesn't serve the same purpose anymore. We don't need it the same way.

If you should fear anything, don't fear failure. Fear regrets for never trying. Fear not saying those important words to someone. Fear living a life without passion.

When it's time to die, we are not sad about what we did. We are sad about what we didn't do. The things we never even gave a chance.

How to Conquer Fear

We have already talked about how fear today is different—it doesn't serve the same purpose. And maybe we can understand this on an intellectual level. But it doesn't mean we will not feel fear. It doesn't mean we will never worry.

Conquering fear is maybe more about accepting it, living with it, and learning how to control it instead of letting it control and paralyze us. Because fear will always show its ugly face. It will never disappear. At least not until we actually do what we fear.

> *"Life begins at the end of your comfort zone."*
> ~ Neale Donald Walsch ~

Still, accepting fear and living with it doesn't help us much. We need some tools to help control it.

First, the best way to fight fear is to act fast. The longer we hesitate, the more fear gets hold of us. But if we are not fast enough, there are other ways to fight it.

Second, some things just happen by themselves, and we cannot do much about them. Aging, natural disasters, and eventual death are some examples. What can we do about them? Nothing. So, when we live with the fear of these things, we will prevent ourselves from living.

Other things don't happen by themselves—we must make them happen. We have to decide something or take action, which means we can control them to a certain extent.

Fearing things long before they could happen is what we call worry. And worrying doesn't really help. Especially worrying about things that we can't control.

> *"If a problem can be solved there is no use*
> *worrying about it. If it can't be solved,*
> *worrying will do no good."*
> ~ Buddhist proverb ~

Third, we can figure out if the fear we are feeling is something that really makes sense. Do we fear something that's quite ridiculous to fear? Or is it justified?

We feel fear in many different situations; in some, it doesn't make sense. We must realize that most of what we fear, the bad outcomes, never come true. And even if they do, most of the time, the change these bad outcomes represent is small, so we shouldn't worry about them.

If we worry about an interview for a job, what happens if we "fail" and don't get the job? Nothing. Life is still the same. It's not a risk unless we have something to lose. If there's only an upside, there's nothing to fear. We will not be killed and eaten by wolves.

In other cases, there might be some consequences, but usually, they are not that bad. We can live with them, and it's just temporary.

Even if the outcome is terrible, remember—very few decisions are final. We can almost always change our minds if we must.

There's really not much to fear. If we think about it and realize that nothing will change for the worse if things don't work out as planned, then there's no reason to feel fear.

Fourth, we must realize that everyone feels fear sometimes. At least the people who step outside their comfort zone. When we live like we think our parents, friends, and society expect us to, never stepping outside our comfort zone, we might not feel that much fear. But, if we do anything outside the ordinary, we will sometimes feel fear because we are doing or changing things that we don't know the outcome of.

Everyone feels fear sometimes. It can also make us feel more alive. Accept it. Embrace it. If other people can face fear, so can you.

Fifth, if we dig a bit deeper, we might understand that fear is telling us something. When we are outside our comfort zone, we are where the magic happens. Outside our comfort zone is where we develop. This is where we grow. It's also where we can find flow.

> *"Move out of your comfort zone. You can only grow if you are willing to feel awkward and uncomfortable when you try something new."*
> ~ Brian Tracy ~

Fear can be our friend. Try to make friends with it because it tells us we are on the way. It might not be the right way. We can never be 100 % sure of that. But we are doing something right. We are growing and developing. We are moving forward.

The trick is to recognize fear as something good. If things don't turn out as we want, we learn something from it. We shouldn't back down as soon as we feel fear. It's better to take it as a signal we might be onto something. Something that, at the very least, makes us grow.

Sixth, challenge fear, and we will get stronger. Fear can be like a thermometer. It will show us how much we will grow when we do whatever is causing it. More fear means we will grow more. We can take it as a challenge. The next time we try to do the same thing, we will feel less of it, even if we failed the first time.

Fear at its highest level comes from our insecurity—that we will not be able to handle it. Action gives us more power. It gives us more confidence. The more we push it, the more we realize we can handle it. The more our confidence grows, the easier it will become to challenge fear the next time. And over time, fear will lose its grip on us.

We also get used to feeling a bit of fear—the sensation. Of course, whenever we get out of our comfort zone, we will feel some fear again. But it gets easier. The more we grow our comfort zone, the less fear we will feel. And the more used to the feeling, the less it can control us.

The best way to fight fear is to do what frightens us as soon as possible. And then do it until we no longer fear it.

We can practice facing our fear daily with ever-so-small actions. Just do something that feels slightly uncomfortable, and slowly the comfort zone will grow.

Finally, we can try to reframe fear. In a way, the fear we feel is a construction of the mind. The feeling of fear is not an inevitable result of something that could happen in the future. It's just our *view* of it. There are other ways of viewing the same future event.

There are several outcomes, and each one will present some new challenges but also some new opportunities. How will you live if you always give in to fear? If you don't follow your passion? If you don't live a life true to yourself? Or, how much worse would life be if you don't go through with whatever change you want to make? Maybe the answers to these questions are more frightening than what you are fearing?

So, we can reframe fear as something preventing us from living our dream life, which sounds much more terrifying to me.

Now or Later?

Humans, in general, love instant gratification. And looking back through history, it made a lot of sense from an evolutionary standpoint.

Things were more challenging then. Eating as much as possible made sense, so we didn't risk losing the chance to eat it later. It made sense to rest now, to save energy when we had the opportunity, in case we might need it later. It made sense to be lazy and eat as much as we could.

It also made sense to have short-term thinking. Throughout history, having goals twenty years, five years, or maybe even one year from now was not as relevant. We might not even be alive by then.

But today, this thinking makes us vulnerable. First of all, we live today, not 50 000 years ago. Things have changed. The dangers are not the same, and we don't need to be well-rested just in case. Now we have the opposite problem—we overeat and move too little. The number of calories we can quickly get our hands on is way higher now.

And secondly, without having a long-term perspective, it's hard for us to see the results of what we do. We know what's here and now. We see the immediate benefit. We experience the pleasures of having a chocolate cake or staying on a comfortable sofa.

In many cases, it's dopamine playing tricks on us. Our bodies are flooded with dopamine when we eat fat and sugar. We are hard-wired to search for that sensation. We search for what gives us that dopamine response. Nowadays, big producers even engineer food to provide us with that response.

Social media, games, etc., are also designed to use this response and keep us hooked. What's more, when we have those high dopamine levels, we more easily fall prey to other temptations. We become even less concerned with the long term. We can't immediately see the impact on our weight, health, or finances. We can't see what exercising will give us in five years. But we can feel how nice it's to stay in bed in the morning, snoozing a bit longer instead of jogging. We can't imagine what just an hour a day on a side hustle could give our life in five years. So, it's easy to convince ourselves, "just this once," "just one more," or "I'll do it tomorrow."

> *The problem isn't telling yourself, "Just this once." The problem isn't saying, "I'll do it tomorrow." The problem is saying, "Just this once" or "I'll do it tomorrow" every day.*

So, we need to pay more attention to the real impact of our daily choices. The true costs. And we must make it clear to ourselves why we shouldn't feed our need for instant gratification.

The only time is now. The only moment we can really live is happening right now. And that's also the only moment we can decide on our future.

> *Where you are doesn't matter. That's a result of the past, and no one can change that. Where you are going is what matters, and that's determined by what you do right now. So, where are you going?*

What we do right now will define our future. So, we must make sure our choices are good. We must stop living through memories of the past or dreams for the future. We have to start living here and now and create our life, whether that means stopping doing something or start doing something. Or doing both.

Choices & Priorities

Life today is a result of all previous choices. Everything we do in life involves some choice, and every choice reflects some priority. If we decide to go to the gym, it's a choice that reflects a priority. If we sit on the sofa and watch TV instead of finishing writing our book, it's a choice that reflects a priority.

If we never make hard choices, we will stay exactly where we are and receive what comes our way. This is just reality.

I often think we don't feel like we made a choice. Time just flew by, and we missed the chance to go to the gym or whatever we would have wanted. But there was a choice. We could have gotten up from the sofa as soon as the thought popped into our head, gathered the gym clothes, and left for the gym, but we didn't.

I have started to live by a new rule. At least I try. I try to include more long-term thinking in my life. Whenever I must make a choice, I try to imagine the results of that choice if I would *always* make that same choice. I multiply the action in my mind. So, I imagine what would happen if I had the same priority and made the same choice for one year? Or five years? What I do today is how I create my future.

Once again, the life we have today is simply a result of all our previous choices. And the life we have one year, or five years from now, will result from all the choices we make from now onwards.

If your life is great, keep doing what you are doing. If you are not happy about some things in life, maybe you need to make some new choices.

We can never be sure of the exact consequences of what we do, but at least we can control our choices.

There's a story about a Tibetan lama speaking to a group of monks. He showed them a jar, put some stones in it, and asked, "Is it full?". Yes, they replied. He then pulled out some gravel, put it in the jar, and shook it a little, so the pieces fell into place in the crevices. Once again, he asked, "Is it full?". "No, probably not," they replied. He took out a bucket of sand and poured some in. The question and answer were repeated. He poured in some water until it was really full. Nothing more could fit in. "What's the point?" he asked. One of the monks replied, "No matter how full your day is, you can always fit something more in." The lama replied—"Good answer! But the point is that if you don't put the rocks in first, you will never fit them in!"

We better find out what's really important in our lives. Which are our "rocks"? What are our priorities? What do we really want? And then we must make sure we fit that in—focus on that first. Only later can we start filling up with other things that might not be as important.

The remarkable thing is that it doesn't need to take very long to change your life. With the right choices, consistency, and the compound effect of time, your life can change in a year, months, or even weeks.

How much we can change will depend on what we want to change, what we have been doing so far, how much effort we are willing to put in, and how consistent we are with those changes.

Sometimes when we make a change in life, it's because we are at a low point. We are in a place where we are unhappy, and we suddenly realize we can't continue further on that road. We must change something. It can be after a long night out drinking. It can be when the scale reaches a certain weight. Or maybe when the bank account runs dry. This is the wake-up call we need—the moment when we suddenly realize what we are doing to ourselves.

So, we decide to change. It can feel fantastic because we love to imagine ourselves in the future. A future when we are already fit, eat well, have a great job, and have healthy finances. We think of a disciplined person who makes all the right decisions. Our future self has all the priorities right, and no temptations are too big. Basically perfect. Imagining ourselves like this gives us hope.

The problem is that we don't live in the future. Our future self does not exist. Deciding to change is far from being that future self. Yes, we might be able to create the perfect self in the future, but we live now, and who makes the choices now is our current, imperfect self. So, we better make sure to get our priorities right so we can make the right decisions already now. We better make sure our present self gets stronger. Our future self will thank us for it.

Input & Output

Whatever we do in life, we will get back. There's a powerful connection between input and output. It's like karma in a way, and it works the same for relationships, our bodies, and our minds. If we give our bodies input in the form of junk food and a lot of sugar, they will give us output that is just as bad. If we feed our minds with soap operas and gossip magazines, they will not produce the best business ideas.

Our minds will work with whatever we feed them. If we give them negativity, they will stay in a negative state.

If you can, avoid the negative news, gossip, and brain-dead tv-shows that show you the misery of other people's lives.

Live your own life instead of looking at others living theirs.

And if you want quality output, feed yourself with quality input.

It has been proven that our five closest friends, the five people we spend the most time with, can predict how successful we are in life, our health, and even our happiness. In short, their level of success predicts our level of success. Their level of health predicts our level of health. Their level of happiness predicts our level of happiness. This tells us a lot about the influence our closest have on us. They can pull us in a different direction. They can inspire us. They can show us new possibilities. So, if we want to change in a positive way, it makes sense to avoid spending too much time with the people who live and breathe negativity. It's contagious. But so is positivity, so we should spend time with people who are positive and push us in a positive direction.

I think this is also true for our role models. Do we follow and admire people who do stupid things in reality TV shows? Or do we try to follow the lead of people who live successful lives trying to make the world a better place?

If we want to make sure our closest have a positive impact on our lives, first, we need to pay attention to what feelings they give us. Do we feel positive or negative around them? Are they talking about solutions and opportunities or mostly about problems and obstacles? The best are the ones who encourage us to be or become our best selves. The people who make us feel more energized when we meet them and who help and support us in reaching our goals.

If you have children old enough to roam the neighborhood, you probably have also developed feelings for their friends. Some of them you like, and others you know will get your sweet kid into trouble. You can feel it instinctively. If you think about it, you can use the same instincts on your own friends.

I have had a couple of relations that were definitely *not* good for me. I knew it somewhere inside. I was gradually feeling worse and worse—totally drained of energy. Sometimes we don't listen to that gut feeling, so it took a long time, and it was difficult, but in the end, I managed to break free. And as soon as I broke free, I could feel the energy flooding back. It was like the relationship had sucked up all my energy—a dam preventing it from flowing. And as soon as I finished it, the dam burst, and my energy came flooding back. Sometimes our work can have the same effect, sucking up our energy.

So, take a look at the people you spend time with. Who is lifting you up? Who inspires you to get better? Who gives you that energy boost when you meet them? Who gives you the courage and determination to keep going? Try to spend more time with those people and maybe add some more of them.

Fill your brain with new ideas, science, research, inspirational books, and biographies of successful people. Learn more about whatever you find interesting. The more we expose ourselves to positivity, the easier it will be to fight off all the negativity we meet in the world.

Once we start to change, we will notice what kind of people surround us. We will see who is supporting us when we change. We will notice who gets happy and inspired and who encourages us. And we will notice who isn't. Some might even try to hold us back or talk us out of things. Maybe because we break the "rules." Perhaps because it feels better to be miserable if others are miserable too. And the more we change, the more resistance we might encounter.

The body and mind are our tools, the machines we have to work with. They will not function optimally if we don't give them the right energy source. If we don't take care of them and service them from time to time, they will fall apart.

This is true for both the body and the mind:

"If you don't use it, you lose it!"

The Key to Success

I hope you know what's really important in your life by now. You are more aware of your desires and clear on what you want in life—what needs to change. You know what you are doing and the results you are getting. You know about the courage, determination, and hard work required to succeed.

But isn't there some little secret? Something that makes it all a bit easier. Yes, there is. We know that what we do daily impacts our lives massively over time.

"We are what we repeatedly do. Excellence, then, is not an act but a habit."
~ Aristotle ~

We are what we repeatedly do and are already creatures of habit. We start our days the same way. We eat the same food. We take the same road to work. We have all kinds of good and bad habits, and some that don't make much of a difference—neither good nor bad. So, if we are already creatures of habit, we just need to make sure we pick the right ones. We can achieve pretty much any result with the right habits.

When we are stressed, we rely even more on habits. So, when we lead a stressful life, we follow even closer to the road they take us. Good habits can save us in those moments because otherwise, the autopilot will take over and lead us in the wrong direction.

This is why we have habits. They make life easier. They make things automatic.

A lot of what we do on any given day is out of habit. When we don't need to think, the brain saves energy. If we had to think about every action we take, we would be too tired already around lunch. So, habits help us a lot, and they are essential if we want to succeed. But even if they can help us, it doesn't mean it's easy. Remember, there are no shortcuts in life.

Brain Plasticity

Brain plasticity sounds a bit complex, but it's less complicated than it seems. It means that the brain is plastic—it can change. The brain is in a certain way and works in a certain way now. We are good or bad at certain things, but we can change. We can get better. We can learn new things. We can rewire the brain.

We become better when we repeatedly do something, and the neural pathways associated with that action become stronger.

That's what happens with habits too. The more times we repeat a behavior, the stronger the neural pathways. It's like a path in the forest. The more we use it, the clearer it will become. The easier it will be to see where it goes and follow it.

If someone has been an office worker all their life and never used their body much, try dancing salsa for the first time, it might be challenging and look stiff and unnatural. But with practice, anyone can learn and improve, thanks to the brain's plasticity. This is why we are good at what we often do and are not very good at what we seldom do.

The stronger neural pathways of our habits are both good and bad. Why? Because it works the same way for both good and bad habits. For the good habits, it's great because it makes it easy for us to keep them. For the bad habits, it's terrible because it's easy to keep them too.

The longer we do something, the stronger the pathway becomes, so the newer habits are easier to break. They don't have as strong pathways yet. If they are good, we must make them stronger through repetition to ensure we keep them. And if they are bad, we must break them quickly before their pathways are too strong.

Compounding Effects of Time

We have already concluded that life right now is the result of our everyday choices. It's not the result of gorging at a single buffet but of what we eat regularly on any typical day. It's not the result of running a marathon but what kind of training we do all year round. And life in the future will result from the habits we keep, the new ones we create, and the ones we choose to quit. A tiny change now can make a huge difference over time if we stick to it. Just like money put in a good investment can grow tremendously over time, our choices will have the same compounding effect. We just need to decide in which direction we want our life to go—up or down.

The fact that one day will not make a difference also means that if we forget or miss doing something one day, it will hardly affect the end result. Unless this miss makes us skip the next day too, and then quit entirely.

Every moment of every day, we have a choice—we can choose to do something that will improve our life or something that won't. Each individual choice can seem very small and insignificant, and results can take some time to see. Still, over time it makes a big difference. So, we must stay on track long enough for the results to show and start compounding. Once we see results, it's always easier to keep going.

Imagine we want to learn French. The best way to learn is to go to France, take a course, read newspapers, magazines, and books, and speak to many people daily. Total immersion is the fastest way to learn any language, but it can also be expensive.

And we need days off work for the trip, during which we will probably not make money as usual.

Another way would be to enroll in a local language course. It's not as expensive and takes just a couple of hours per week, but we will have to do it for a more extended period if we want similar results. There are a lot of obstacles—the timing might not be good, it might not fit into our schedule, and the price might put us off. What if we miss one or two classes and feel behind in class? There are several reasons not to start and other reasons to quit.

But what if we buy a cheap app for our phone and then practice vocabulary every time we commute to work? Let's say we have 30 minutes one way. We will spend an hour per day in total. That's five hours per week. Probably more hours than we would do in a local course. In a year, that's around 260 hours or 6,5 weeks of full-time studies.

What did we lose? Not much money for the app, and then we missed the immense joy of some random scrolling on Facebook or the social media app of choice. Nothing we will miss in the long run. Nothing that would have helped us achieve any important goals in life.

What would the results be? How many new words could we learn in 6,5 weeks of full-time studying? I bet we would have a fully working vocabulary and have pinned down most of the grammar we need to make ourselves understood. Add another language to the CV!

Or imagine we are very curious and want to learn many different things. So, we decide to read non-fiction books instead of scrolling social media. A one-hour commute every day would equal some 40-60 pages. Let's say an average non-fiction book contains 200-300 pages; then it's one book per week or more than 50 books in a year. Imagine how much more we would learn in just a year. And in ten years, that's 500 books. All that instead of some social media scrolling.

If we take another example of the compounding effects of time, imagine just skipping a 100-gram chocolate bar once a week. One bar contains around 520 calories. In a year, we multiply those by the 52 weeks, and we get 27 040 calories. Since one kilo of fat is 7778 calories, we get to just about 3,5 kilos of fat. In ten years, that small change—one chocolate bar per week— could save us from 35 kilos of excess weight. Those 35 kilos would not be a walk in the park to get rid of. Imagine the difference we could make if we skip not just one chocolate bar per week but all sweets and products with added sugar.

In addition, *not* having that extra weight on the body might prevent us from saying "what the hell" before we allow ourselves a second chocolate bar per week. Feeling bad for oneself tends to have that effect—that we fall for temptations more easily.

Not having it can also make it much more likely that we will get outside to do some exercise occasionally. Because having a lot of extra fat makes getting started and the workout much more challenging.

We have already seen what changed habits and sustained effort can achieve over time, thanks to the compounding effects of time. And this is without even considering the positive secondary effects that a change in one area can have on other areas of life.

THE SOLUTION TO OUR PROBLEMS

The Brain & its Functions

There are two main systems in our brain, and two different parts of the brain are responsible for them.

The first one we will talk about is the basal ganglia. It's approximately the size of a golf ball and is placed in the center of the skull. This is the part of the brain responsible for our automated actions. The things we do without thinking. You could say it's a bit stupid but also swift and reliable. Kind of like a stupid friend who doesn't think much of the consequences. It does whatever feels right at the moment, trying to protect you. And it repeats actions unless we actively try to prevent them. The basal ganglia are very much here and now. No thinking about the future. This is where we find our automatic responses to the patterns we recognize and recall. Therefore, we also find our habits here.

When our brain tries to save energy, it relies on something called "chunking," trying to convert a behavioral sequence into an automatic routine. Once the automated routine is in place, the brain saves energy.

The second part we will talk about is the prefrontal cortex. This is the part of our brain that's specifically human in that no other species has a prefrontal cortex as developed as we do. This is the part of the brain we use to think long-term and where we can actually evaluate options—where we can weigh pros and cons. It's more analytical and the part we use to think about the future. It helps us control our immediate desires, it helps us delay gratification, and it protects our more long-term goals.

These two parts constantly interact, but as you can imagine, they don't always agree. It's like having two friends who want what's good for you but have very different mindsets. There's a "battle" going on between them. The brain typically wants to save energy, directing as many tasks as possible to the basal ganglia. It wants us to act out of habit. It wants us to do things without thinking about them, just to save energy. But sometimes, when there's no recognizable pattern, the brain must engage our prefrontal cortex and think through our choices a bit more. This takes more energy, but it can save us in many situations.

When it comes to our habits, if we want to create a new one, we try to consciously engage in a behavior enough times to make it automatic. Once it is, the brain can delegate the decision to the basal ganglia.

And suppose we want to break a habit. In that case, we want to do the opposite—make the behavior more conscious and elevate the decision to the prefrontal cortex.

How Habits Work

We all know what habits are. But maybe we don't know much about them—how they are formed, how we can get rid of them, and so on. We don't give them that much thought.

A habit can be our best friend and our worst enemy. Since it's something we do practically every time we are in a particular situation, it can be very powerful. Especially since a big part of our day is made of habits.

To engage in a behavior, we need some type of motivation. We need a trigger, and we need the ability to do it. Without enough motivation, we will not do it. Without a trigger, we will not do it. And without enough ability, we will not be able to do it, even if we have the first two.

The motivation and the ability interact. If we have very low motivation, it must be effortless to engage in the behavior. And if it's challenging to do, we need a lot of motivation.

One way in which habits save us energy is through "chunking," which is also part of how habits form. We prepare the coffee, and we drink the coffee in one sequence—or chunk. Our conscious brain, the prefrontal cortex, can relax when we work in habit mode.

This is extremely helpful if the habits are good. It can also be terrible if they are bad. Or it can be quite neutral if the habits are neutral—like when we flip out the phone and scroll a bit on Instagram while on the subway. But we will talk more about neutral habits later.

When we are just starting to create a habit, there's a decision behind it. We have to engage our prefrontal cortex. But the more we engage in that behavior, the less of a conscious effort it becomes. The more automatic it gets.

If we are going to break them down a bit more, habits consist of four things:

- The reminder—a trigger or cue. This is what starts the loop. It can be pretty much anything, a time of day, a visual trigger, a place, a person, a feeling, or a thought. From now on, I will use the word "trigger" since "reminder" has a connotation of something more conscious. Trigger sounds more like on autopilot—what habits are like.
- The craving—a desire for a reward. This motivates us to act, but it doesn't have to feel like a real craving. It isn't necessarily like an addiction. It can be barely noticeable.
- The routine—a specific behavior we perform as a response to the trigger, so we can get the reward. This is what we are after—the actual behavior we will work with, whether to create a habit or quit one.
- The reward—a benefit we receive from engaging in the behavior. This can also be a lot of different things, psychological or physical.

Altogether this sequence will create a positive or a negative feedback loop. If it's positive, there will be a stronger drive to repeat the same behavior the next time we experience the same trigger. And the opposite is also true.

The habit results from many conscious decisions, which over time will make us perform the behavior without thinking about it, if it's a positive feedback loop. The loop only repeats if the brain gets a reward—something that makes it want to repeat the behavior the next time we are in that situation. When we repeat the behavior, the brain starts to change. Since the brain resists change, this change doesn't happen directly. But certain areas connected to the behavior start activating, and the neural pathways associated with that behavior become stronger. The stronger they become, the stronger the habit will be. Once the brain can automate things this way, it can save energy, and we can focus on other, more complicated problems we need to solve.

During this habit loop, the brain is more active in the beginning, during the trigger phase. It tries to recognize which pattern to use. Once it has found the correct one, it relaxes again. It saves energy until the reward comes. Then it's once again activated to finish the loop, check off the result and decide what to do next. Either it searches for a new trigger to engage in another habitual behavior, or it activates the prefrontal cortex to engage in some more conscious thought.

There are many different theories of how long it takes to create a habit. Some say 21 days, others say 30, and yet others say it's more than 100 days. In reality, it depends a lot on what behavior it is and more on the number of times that behavior is performed than the exact number of days. Some habits will form faster, and some will develop slower.

In a way, I think that discussion is meaningless because it's not like forming a habit is something that happens from one day to the other. It's not like we are trying to build it for 59 days, and then on the 60th day, it's all of a sudden all set. It's a process. It happens over time, slowly but surely, if we are consistent. Day ten of trying to form a habit will feel easier than day two. Day 30 will feel easier than day ten, and so on. And if we would miss a day, it's less risky to do so after 30 days than after five days. The new neural pathways have already become more robust, and we don't risk losing them as easily. So, it's crucial that we don't stop, even if we miss a day. Another reason it doesn't matter exactly how long it takes to form the habit is that the goal is not just to make it a habit. The goal is to get the results the behavior gets us. And we usually want those results for life, so precisely when they have become a habit is unimportant.

Once the habit is formed, the neurological response can start appearing even before the actual reward. This is because we begin anticipating the reward. And we repeat the behavior because we start craving the result.

When we see a deliciously looking brownie, we anticipate the taste and sugar rush and buy it. The brain adapts to this, and if the reward wasn't as big for some reason, we would get disappointed or annoyed.

Imagine a brownie that looks mouth-wateringly calorie-dense—full of sugar and fat—and then when you taste it, it's nothing of the sort. Maybe bark bread would be an exaggeration, but dry and tasteless is not unlikely. Now that would be a turn-off if anything. We wouldn't buy that brownie again. We wouldn't even crave it, and craving is an essential element in creating a habit.

Suppose the reward doesn't come at all. In that case, we show neurological patterns of desire and frustration, just like we would have in the bad brownie example above.

The right trigger and the proper reward aren't quite enough. The craving drives the loop. It's only when we start expecting and craving the reward that it becomes a fully formed and powerful habit, even if the craving is hardly noticeable.

Still, it's a loop—a chain of events—and we need all the links. And for good or bad, this chain can be pretty weak. If there's a slight change in one of the links, it can break.

Now that we know this process, we can observe how habits form and learn how to better control them. We can create new habits, and we can break old ones.

Keystone Habits

We know habits are powerful tools to change our lives, but some habits are so powerful that they cause a domino effect that ripples through our lives. They start a chain reaction—one small change creates new changes and can turn into a total life transformation. These powerful habits are called keystone habits.

Take exercise, for example. When we start working out and manage to make it into a habit, we often start eating better as a result. Then we start sleeping better due to both exercise and better nutrition. With better physique, sleep, and nutrition, we become more productive at work. We might get more positive feedback when we are more productive at work. We might also get a promotion or a raise as a nice benefit. Together all these changes make us feel happier. And when we are happier, it affects our relationships.

It's a chain reaction set in motion by one small change—starting to exercise.

Getting a keystone habit in place can be the domino that kicks it all off. It can really help us start other good habits, transforming life in the process.

Good, Bad, & Neutral Habits

All habits fall on a scale from good to bad, but if we generalize, we can divide habits into three distinct categories—good habits, bad habits, and neutral habits. We all have some good and some bad ones. The neutral ones are the ones that don't make that much of a difference.

The problem is that our brains can't distinguish between habits if they are good or bad. Yes, we can figure it out on a conscious level, but not on that subconscious level where habits rule.

I would define a good habit as something that improves the quality of life in some way. It can be about health, relationships, or finances, for example. Getting a body with a healthy fat percentage, a happy marriage, or a higher salary are all results of good habits. A bad habit will make the quality of life worse in some way. It might lead to obesity, create a toxic relationship, or a lost job.

The problem with good and bad habits is that the behavior often feels one way here and now but creates a different outcome over time. Good habits are usually not very pleasurable right now, but they have a positive long-term effect. Bad habits are the opposite—they are pleasurable now but have a negative long-term effect.

Good habits are often easy to quit because it's pleasurable now. And bad habits are difficult to quit for the same reason. They are pleasurable here and now.

Unfortunately, humans have evolved to search for this instant gratification. We look for it because, for a long time, it was better for our survival. It was always best to eat now if we wanted to be sure to eat. If we tried to save it for later, we could lose the opportunity. But today's environment is totally different, creating other problems—now we can usually eat both now and later.

Our third category—the neutral habit—is neither good nor bad. It's something we do that neither improves our quality of life nor makes it worse in any significant way. Time in front of the TV will not do much good, but not much harm either.

So far, I think we can agree that we should aim to break bad habits and create good new ones if we want to improve life. But it also makes sense to think about neutral habits like scrolling our social media, binge-watching TV, or reading gossip online. They are not good or bad, really. Or are they?

We can't do everything. Whatever we decide to do has a cost—the cost of missing out on what we could have done instead. When we say yes to something unimportant, we also say no to something else. Maybe something important.

In microeconomic theory, there's the concept of opportunity cost. From the definition on Wikipedia, we can learn that:

"In microeconomic theory, the opportunity cost of a particular activity is the value or benefit given up by engaging in that activity, relative to engaging in an alternative activity."

We have a limited amount of time. We can't do all that we want. We must choose. So, if we spend our day in front of the TV, we miss out on all the benefits we could have gotten from other, more productive ways of spending the day. Neutral habits are not harmful in themselves, but compared to good habits, they are.

I am not saying that we should never relax. On the contrary, we all need to get some time when we are not "working" our brain or body. But if we spend a lot of time on these neutral habits, which don't really contribute to improving life, we will have to accept that life doesn't advance very much either. It will stay the same—neutral. It will not have the quality it could have. It's really that simple.

So, if we look back at the examples we used earlier in this book:

- If we keep scrolling on social media, we miss out on 6,5 weeks of studying French, probably making us able to speak it reasonably well, or:
- We miss out on the knowledge gained from 50 books in a year or 500 books in ten years!

Quitting bad habits and limiting neutral habits could make a massive difference if we take care of the time saved. It could turn us into someone who makes passive income and works a 10-hour work week from anywhere in the world instead of being stuck in our 9-5 job.

Life right now is a result of the habits we have had up until now. Life in the future will be the result of the habits we keep from now on. And replacing a few bad and neutral habits with some good ones can make a big difference.

Quitting Bad Habits or Starting Good Ones?

I believe that if we want to create a great life, in many cases, it makes sense to first look at our bad habits before we start building good new ones. I believe it could be the fastest way to improve life. Why? Because maybe they will affect the likelihood we will succeed with good habits. Remember keystone habits?

Some bad habits are like negative keystone habits—they make it more challenging to create change.

Let's take an example with someone who eats decent, smokes, and doesn't exercise. This person wants to improve their health, so they want to start jogging every morning. To me, it would make more sense to stop smoking before starting jogging. Why? Because smoking will make it much more challenging to stick to the new habit of jogging every morning.

Just eight hours after the last cigarette, both nicotine and carbon monoxide levels in the blood are reduced by half, and oxygen levels are back to normal. After 48 hours, nicotine and carbon monoxide are gone from the body. This means the potential uptake of oxygen is much higher. Lungs are starting to clear from mucus and other debris from smoking. So, breathing will be much easier and more efficient. And all this also means jogging will be much easier.

In just 8 hours, they will have an easier time getting oxygen to the muscles, and in two days, every breath will be very different. It will be so much easier to start jogging every morning. This means it will also be much easier to make it a habit.

Another example could be our finances. If we want better finances, there are two ways we can go about it. Either we can make more money. This usually requires building some good habits. Or we can spend less, which probably requires quitting reckless spending habits.

Which one makes an impact instantly? It's to cut spending. Making more money can be challenging, and it usually takes time. Spending less is instantaneous and probably also easier.

The last example is weight. Eating less is much easier to do than exercising more. Imagine that 100-gram chocolate bar. It has 520 calories. That's at least 30 minutes of running, but it depends on our weight and speed. It could be as low as 280 calories for 30 minutes of running. So, it could almost take as much as one hour of running to burn the chocolate bar. Avoiding the chocolate bar is more manageable than an hour of running, at least, I think so.

So, I believe that eliminating bad habits often has a more profound and quicker effect on life, and it's worth thinking about before we decide what we start with.

And when we are creating good habits or quitting bad ones and want to change several things, it can be wise to start with the easy ones. This helps us build momentum and confidence, making it much easier to continue.

How to Quit a Bad Habit

To start or stop doing anything, first, we need to believe we can make it. It's the same with habits. We need to believe we can do it. If we feel convinced enough, then we are ready. If we don't believe it, we will not really make enough effort.

Let's say we have identified some bad habits. What's next? We want to get rid of them, of course. And since they are something we have learned, they can also be unlearned. But first, we need to make the decision to change, and we need to make a conscious effort to do so. The fact that it's a habit means the behavior has been automated, so now we need to short-circuit that process.

A habit means there are neural pathways in the brain structure that will stay forever, even if they become less prominent over time when we quit. So, it's not like changing a light bulb. It's not like the habit is gone forever. The right trigger can still make us engage in the old behavior. So, we have to watch out, so we don't slip.

When we want to quit a habit, first, we need to figure out the loop that drives it, and the most obvious component of the loop is the behavior we want to quit. This is our starting point, but what else is there?

The first step in the habit loop is the trigger. If we want to short-circuit the loop, the trigger can be critical. This requires some awareness. Is it a person? Is it a situation? Is it a feeling? Is it a specific place? Is it a particular time of day? If this is hard to figure out, we can try to take note every time we start engaging in the bad habit.

- Where are we?
- Who is around?
- What time is it?
- What kind of situation is it?
- How did we feel just before?
- What happened just before?

If we find the trigger, we can try to eliminate it. This is probably the easiest way to quit a bad habit because it requires no willpower or extra effort later. We simply remove the trigger, and the loop doesn't start.

Hide what triggers the behavior. We don't diet at home; we diet when buying groceries. If we don't have chocolates and sweets at home, we will not snack on them because there are no reminders that trigger the snacking behavior. So, if we eat a lot of chocolate at home because we see it every day and fall for the temptation—clean the house of chocolate and don't buy any more. Eliminating the reminder is one way of kicking a habit. Of course, if it's a person who's the reminder, it might be more sensitive to eliminate them from life.

Another option is to avoid the trigger—we don't go to where we experience the trigger. We don't meet people who will remind us. Whatever it is, avoid it.

A third option is to ignore the reminder, but it's not always easy and requires us to be strong. If we can neither eliminate, avoid, or ignore it, we must try something else.

The second step in the loop is the craving. It appears because we associate the reward with the behavior. To short-circuit the loop at this stage requires reframing what the response will give us.

If we go back to the chocolate example, from now on, "chocolate is making me fat." If we think of spending on unnecessary lattes, from now on, "lattes are ruining me." If we want to quit watching reality shows on TV, from now on, they "stop me from working on my passion and be able to live my dream life in five years." We must make the bad habit seem to have terrible consequences because it probably does, at least in the long run.

The third step in the loop is the routine. We already know this because it's the behavior we want to quit. To say we should simply stop makes it seem more straightforward than it is. But one way we can make it easier is to make it more difficult. Did that sound strange? Yes, it did. I mean this: one way of making it easier to quit the behavior is to make it more difficult to engage in it. We can do this by increasing how much time it requires, how much it costs, or the physical or mental effort. If we can't tear ourselves from the TV set at night, set a timer in the outlet to the TV electrical cord, and it will shut off at whatever time we want. Or, if we absolutely need to have peanut butter at home but want to stop eating a spoonful every time we pass the kitchen, then we can put it in the freezer. When we really need it for something, we have to plan for it and take it out in time. But we can't keep snacking on it when we pass the kitchen. It's frozen, and we don't want the hassle of unfreezing it. So, we skip snacking.

Nowadays, technology makes many things easier, but technology can also be used to make things more difficult. Some apps let us keep track of our web surfing or even limit it if we want. There are apps for everything, also for helping us keep track of new habits or quit bad ones. We should take advantage of technology when we can.

Another way to quit a bad habit at this stage would be to replace the bad routine with another routine—we create a "competing response." This requires some more thinking. To change an old habit, we need to handle the craving. We need to figure out what satisfies us—what are we after? We need to find the habit's real reward, which might not be so obvious. What do we really crave? Is it the nicotine rush or the small break from work? Is it the rush of the online game, or an escape from life's problems? Is it hunger, or just that we are bored?

Then we need to substitute the routine for our competing response while still making sure the craving for the reward is satisfied. The new routine needs to satisfy the same craving, preferably better than the old one, so it motivates us enough. It needs to meet the same needs without giving us harmful effects.

And it also needs to be easy to do, preferably easier to do than the old habit.

Once we know the reward we seek, we can try to override the automatic response and instead insert the new routine. Between the trigger and the routine, there's a short moment where we can try to intervene and choose what to do. But this requires a conscious effort.

So, we must develop a plan for what we will do once we feel the craving or notice we are about to start. Something that's not as bad as the previous routine.

The key here is awareness. When we notice we feel the desire, when we feel the craving, we can try to take a step back and pause. Try to make the decision more conscious. Identify the trigger and the reward but try to force a different response with the new routine. One way is to stop for a minute or two and just relax. We can try to notice what's happening, and then it's easier to make a conscious decision on what to do instead. Override the autopilot. Over time we will have created a new pattern and replaced the old habit with a new one—with a stronger neural pathway. It's a new habit but feeding off the same trigger and the same reward.

Some people prefer to quit a habit immediately. Others prefer to slow down

or cut back and gradually make the shift. Cutting back can make it a bit easier for some since the part of us that wants to keep the habit doesn't freak out. I know what works best for me but do whatever works best for you.

It's also possible to shift one habit at a time, just as some people choose to change several at the same time. It depends a bit on how fast results we want, our willpower, our level of motivation, and the belief that we can change.

That belief can also come from people around us, the people we surround ourselves with. Or maybe it comes from a role model. Someone we look up to. Someone who has made the change we are about to make. Believing we can change makes all the difference. And that belief is often facilitated within a group.

If it's tough, search for people with a similar challenge. People who want to achieve the same or a similar change. Somewhere someone out there wants to make that change. Somewhere someone out there has *already* tried to make that change and succeeded. You can too!

How to Start a Good Habit

We know how to quit a habit, but how do we create one? We have already learned that a behavior needs to be repeated many times to become a habit. It's not so much about the time spent trying to create it but more about the number of times we manage to follow through.

Before anything else, we need to be sure that the habit we think of creating will help. We need to pick behaviors that will have a high level of impact to help us achieve our goal.

The characteristics we are looking for are; easy to do, that we want to do, and that they effectively achieve our goal. If it's neither easy nor likely we will do them, the chances of creating a habit are slim. We want to make it easy so that we don't feel like a failure when we engage in the behavior the first time. Then we will fear it less, and it will be easier to do. If we feel successful, we will be more motivated to do it again the next time.

Even though a habit in itself is very subconscious, creating it is a very conscious effort. We learned earlier that we need to believe we are the kind of person who can change. Once we believe that, it will all be more straightforward. And the longer we keep doing it, the more it becomes part of who we are. So:

- Decide the person you want to be.
- Through your behavior, start proving to yourself you are this person.

We also need to know that in the beginning, we must actively make the decision every time. We must pay the mental price here and now to make it automatic later. This can be a heavy price since many people start the change but give up before creating the habit.

Just to review, a habit works like this:

- The trigger—what starts the loop. It can be pretty much anything, a time of day, a visual trigger, a place, a person, a feeling, or a thought.
- The craving—a desire for a reward. This motivates us to act, but it doesn't have to feel like a real craving. It isn't necessarily like an addiction. It can be barely noticeable.
- The routine—a specific behavior we perform as a response to the trigger, so we can get the reward. This is what we are after—the actual behavior we will work with, whether to create a habit or quit one.
- The reward—a benefit we receive from engaging in the behavior. This can also be a lot of different things, psychological or physical.

Many people fail when trying to create new habits, but some things can help us make them much more manageable.

We need to put the reminder in place. We need to know what routine to perform. And to make it more likely we will perform this routine, we need to make it easy for us to engage in the behavior to keep the consistency. We must have a certain level of ability and motivation. The lower the motivation, the higher the ability we must have.

So, if it's incredibly boring, the likelihood we will succeed goes down a lot. If it's fun, we are more likely to succeed. And the lower the ability we have, the higher the motivation we need. We must consider this when we pick the exact behavior we want to make into a habit.

Finally, there needs to be some reward, and the brain must start anticipating and craving that reward for it to become automatic. We always change easier and quicker if we feel good about it.

Over time, if we complete this routine enough times, the brain will start anticipating the result and crave the reward. That's when it has become a habit.

Now we will dive deeper into how we can make it all easier.

HOW TO MAKE CHANGE EASY

Triggers

If there's no trigger, we will not get the impulse to engage in the behavior, and therefore there will be no habit formed. Even with a trigger in place, there will be no behavior if we are not motivated enough or don't have enough ability. So, when we design our habits, we always have to include a clear trigger and be thoughtful about how we create it to maximize our chances.

So, first of all, a trigger cannot be so subtle we don't notice it. It has to be clear what's going on and what it means. Second, the trigger should occur at the right time to increase motivation and ability. Third, the trigger should also happen as close as possible to where we want to engage in the behavior. And fourth, matching the frequency of the trigger with how often we want to engage in the behavior is also a good design.

And finally, if we match the purpose of a habit with the trigger, it can also help, so we might use our morning stretch as a trigger for our ab workout, for example.

Triggers can come in many different forms, but we can sort them into three main categories:

- Person Triggers: These are bodily urges like sleeping, eating, etc., and we usually have a lot of habits around these triggers.

‣ Action Triggers: The habits we already engage in can be excellent triggers. Maybe this is the best type. We just need to find what old behavior the new one matches best with in terms of frequency, timing, motivation level, ability level, proximity, and maybe purpose.

‣ Context Triggers: These can be in the form of a calendar, text message, sticky notes, or notifications. Making too many of these can get a bit overwhelming, though.

That was a bit of an introduction to triggers. Now we will take a closer look at some aspects of them.

Visibility & Timing

Remembering to do something isn't as easy as we could hope when we have a busy schedule. So, creating visible reminders is an intelligent way to help us remember. Putting a note on the door, bathroom mirror, fridge, or similar places is excellent. These are places we regularly see, and they are natural parts of our day.

The note creates a visual reminder that helps us keep on the right track. The more visible the reminders, the more likely we will not forget. Another visual trigger could be when we keep the things we need to engage in the behavior more visible. Kind of like keeping the barbells in plain sight, as opposed to in a box in the wardrobe. The workout is more likely to happen when we regularly see the barbells. Another example could be keeping a jar of water on the kitchen table to make us remember to drink more water.

Another standard tool is using a specific time of day as a reminder to help create a habit. Then the opportunity to do it is built into our daily schedule—like an alarm that goes off at the same time every day, and then we do what we are supposed to do.

"At 8 in the morning, I will do X."

During winter in Sweden, it gets pretty dark. When it's dark, we often don't get enough vitamin D, so I take some supplements. But for a long time, I forgot to take them. They were there in the cupboard. Available, but out of sight. I hadn't put them in the right place.

However, when I moved them to just in front of my coffee capsules, I noticed them daily while preparing my morning coffee. Since I don't miss my coffee in the morning, it was an easy fix to make, and now I take my vitamin D every morning.

Designing our environment to help create certain habits and break others is really effective. And just like in my vitamin D example, we can also use old habits as cues to trigger new ones. I think this is so good it's worth discussing more.

Current Habits & Events

Using current habits to form new ones is one of my best tools. A big part of our lives is just one habit after another. What we just did decides what we do next. Finishing one habit loop becomes the trigger for the next. This might be especially true for morning and evening routines. It's simple to anchor the new behavior to an old habit we already have.

If you want to create some new habits, try to list the things you already do every day and every week. Also, list the things that just happen every day and every week. Then you try to place the new behavior you want to make into a habit connected to one of the old habits you already have. Or in connection with some event that happens at the frequency you want for the new habit.

Where would it be easiest to place it? Place it where it's most likely to succeed — when motivation and ability are high. What time of day is best? How often do you want to do it? Where is the best location for the trigger? And maybe even match the purpose.

With the right trigger, creating a habit becomes much more manageable.

Proximity

We talked a little about proximity, but there's more to say. If we can do something independently of where we are, it's much easier for us to do it. Being limited to a specific place makes it more complicated. But it's not only the limitation that makes it less likely we will do something. The proximity to that place makes a huge difference.

Let's say we have signed up for a class at the gym at 4 PM, and the gym is a 30-minute drive away, without traffic. The class is one hour. With the time for parking, changing clothes, etc., we are looking at maybe two and a half hours in total if there's no traffic. A significant investment of time and potentially quite a hassle to get there. Add to that the risk of missing out if there's too much traffic and we run late. If anything doesn't go as planned, we might miss that workout. It requires a lot of time, and we can never be sure we will make it, even if we try. The brain will have no problem inventing excuses not to go.

Compare that to a simple workout we can do in our own home or anywhere else for 30 minutes. One-fifth of the time required, and available 24/7. There are fewer possible excuses. Of course, there are benefits of scheduled appointments too. For one, they are just that—scheduled, which makes them more likely to happen. Intensity levels in group classes might be higher, and there's a possibility of being pushed harder by the coach. But everything else equal, a more significant investment of time or the need to move to a specific location makes it less likely something will happen. The best workout is the one we do.

So, to use time and space to your advantage—when you sign up for a gym, make sure it's either close to home or work or at least on the way between them. Preferably it should be without the need for any other transportation than walking.

If you want to work out at home, make sure it's easy to start by making your equipment easily accessible, maybe even within sight. Whatever habit you want to create, if you use time and space intelligently, you increase the chances of success.

Small Steps

We have covered different ways of making creating a habit easier. Still, if there's one thing that I think is fundamental to success, it's the one we will cover here.

Have you ever tried anything like this:

‣ Promised yourself you would *only* eat healthy food
‣ Decided to do a one-hour workout every weekday
‣ Told yourself to study something for at least one hour every day
‣ Planned to work on your side hustle for at least two hours every evening

Well, did you manage to create that habit and keep it? Likely, you didn't. Why? Maybe you weren't motivated enough. Perhaps too many other obligations came in between. Or maybe, just maybe, because it was too big of a change. It came too suddenly, and the load was too much to carry. In short, the "obstacle" to start doing it was too big. Too many ways it could fail. There were too many possible excuses.

It's not always about us—how we are. It can also be the way we try to do things. We want to change a lot at once because it makes sense. The more we do, the faster we will change, right? We love the idea of this big change. That one defining moment which will change our life.

Maybe January 1st—the start of a new year—the birth of a new me. Just the act of making the decision makes us feel good. And deciding to make a big change makes us feel even *better*. Making a small change is slow and ineffective if the goal is big, right?

Wrong. One of the most significant obstacles to lasting change is the misconception that we must make it big.

The problem is this: when the change we want to make is big, the obstacle to following through is also considerable. The bigger the change, the more friction to do it. There are too many possible excuses, and when the brain has many possible excuses, it starts to reason whether to do it or not.

With a lot of possible excuses, we will not engage in the behavior enough times. The whole plan starts falling apart, and we won't get the consistency we need. And as a result, we don't create the habit.

"80 percent of success is showing up"
~ Woody Allen ~

It usually requires higher ability if we want to do a lot of something. If we don't have the level of ability to make it easy, we will have to rely on either motivation or willpower to get it done. And since we must engage our brain in the decision, if the motivation isn't strong enough, we will have to use willpower. Whenever we use that, we make a "withdrawal" from our "willpower account" (soon more about that). The bigger this "withdrawal," the quicker our account will run dry.

Another problem is that results usually take time. Even if we would succeed in working out for an hour every day for a whole week, the results will not show yet. The feedback is not very good, and motivation goes down when there's no visible change. This is one of the reasons why people fail when changing habits. They make a big commitment, start to change, fail to see results fast enough, and then give up. They made it too hard, and the rewards were too small.

But there's another way.

Action always beats inaction. Great intentions mean nothing if you don't do anything about them.

Truth be told, big intentions that aren't followed up by action will harm our own self-esteem. We will feel worse because we didn't follow through. Maybe we slip once, then we start slipping more and more, and then we give up. Our self-esteem suffers, and our identity changes towards a "non-finisher."

I have tried the big changes too; for me, they rarely work. The most crucial thing when trying to create a new habit is consistency. If we want to give ourselves the best chance to stay consistent, it's better to start small. It doesn't sound very cool, but it's sustainable. And sustainability gives us the consistency we need to succeed.

> *"A journey of a thousand miles*
> *begins with a single step."*
> ~ Confucius ~

I changed my approach a while ago when I wanted to learn a language. I had already read about habits and understood what I needed to learn. I also downloaded a habit app to keep track of my progress.

When I was setting up my new language learning task in the app, I decided the goal should be to spend just five minutes daily. I don't know why I picked five minutes. Five minutes is almost nothing. It doesn't seem to be enough to learn a language. I mean, how much can you retain in five minutes? Well, it turns out we do learn some if we do it every day. And that's not the most important thing. I realized that if I wanted to make it a habit, it made sense to set the target very low. Five minutes was perfect.

The best practice or exercise is the one you do. The best amount is the amount you finish. Over and over again.

Most important was not the time I spent each session but that I created the habit. Goals should be reasonable and achievable, and if we want to create a habit, it makes sense to have a small goal that creates a tiny obstacle. Something that we can do every day.

That was the first benefit of this approach. Each small decision to start was a no-brainer. The language app was built so that every lesson was five more words, which took five more minutes of my life. It was effortless to start because we have many five-minute opportunities every day. And once I had broken down the initial resistance to starting a language learning session—once I was sitting there studying—it was straightforward to continue. So, after a couple of easy decisions on five more words, I spent, on average, around 30 minutes every day instead of the five I had promised myself to do.

That was the second benefit—momentum kept me going for longer. I reached further than my original goal. No matter how small the goal was initially, I accomplished it and did some more. So, I felt even better than I would have, had I just achieved my initial goal. I was breeding success. And that feeling built my confidence, contrary to what we do when we make big commitments that are broken. Those tend to lead to feelings of guilt or of being inadequate.

So, I created the habit. I could pick up my phone and finish my daily task on the subway or anytime during the day when I had some free time on my hands. It was even possible to do it during commercial breaks on TV. Just turn the volume down and finish the daily task.

It's better to start small. There's nothing special about it. Nothing else is different. It's just easier.

Instead of studying vocabulary for one hour, the goal is five minutes. Instead of writing one chapter of a book, the goal is to sit down and write a paragraph. Instead of two hours of side hustling every day, the goal is to sit down and send five emails or do five phone calls. Instead of a one-hour workout, the goal is ten sit-ups. If it takes less than 5-10 minutes, it's easy to do. Resistance is minimal, and there's no excuse not to start when we can finish so fast.

Actually, we would almost feel ashamed *not* to do it. So, our pride practically forces us. Once we are there doing the sit-ups, just as with language learning, it's effortless to do more than the goal we set.

Some mornings we will feel like not doing anything, but then we do the ten anyway because it's so easy. Sometimes, or maybe most of the time, we will do more once we are already on the floor and have finished the ten. That's great! But remember, it still has to be ok to do just what we set as a goal.

So, we need to find the right size—something that makes it incredibly easy to do—that gives no resistance. There can be no reason to activate the brain and decide whether we should do it, no reason to think we can do it later, and no great willpower to get started. No excuses. Just do it.

The ultimate goal can still be significant. It's just that we break it up into these small things that we can do every day. It's still powerful when we really do it. And the mind will reward us. We will feel great.

Once the habit is established, we can decide to extend it. We can require more. But we should probably keep it small for a long time. And when we increase it, we should only do it until the edge of what still feels comfortable and easy. It's more important to keep consistency. Even if we forget about it and only remember just before bedtime, it should still be possible to do.

And it should always be ok to do just the amount we decided. No need to do "extra" every day. It's ok to do the minimum as long as we do it.

Over time, we can do one hour every day and maintain consistency. That's great! Progress will be faster! But there's a big "*if.*" Don't trade that progress for possible failure and breaking the habit. One final reason to start small is that it has the additional benefit of being much easier to pick up again *if* we get off track.

Just focus on here and now to reach your goal today. Direction is more important than speed. Do something that makes you better every day.

It's a way of thinking, of being. To continually move forward, learning and adapting what we do and how we do it. If we think of it as a destination, we might risk stopping when we reach it. It's better to take it one day at a time and keep going.

Focus on what you are doing here and now, not what you have here and now. Are you taking steps in the right direction? If you are, you are doing the right thing. You might not have what you want yet, but you are doing what's right.
Just be patient.

What you are doing, does it have a positive impact? Where is the arrow pointing, up or down? The results will come if the arrow is pointing up. Just be patient.

> *"We cannot do great deeds unless we are willing to do the small things that make up the sum of greatness."*
> ~ Theodore Roosevelt ~

Rewards

Sometimes the results we get are rewards in themselves, and we tend to repeat a behavior when rewarded for it. Especially if the reward is immediate, the connection in the brain is faster and more robust. The feeling of success is maybe the best reward of them all.

Unfortunately, the real results often come much later. In these cases, it can make sense to help out a bit. We can strengthen the brain connection by creating a more attractive and immediate reward.

In psychology, it's called "conditioning"—when we learn to associate certain behaviors with something positive or negative. We want to make the rewards as attractive as possible for good behavior. And for bad behavior, we want to make them less attractive.

When the result of our behavior is far in the future, it can be nice to reward ourselves with something extra, to get some little treat for our efforts.

It should be something positive and immediately pleasurable that satisfies us somehow. Something that can create the craving necessary to make the habit stick. If we feel good afterward, there's a higher likelihood we will do it again.

This reward could be anything we enjoy, except giving ourselves a break from the habit we want to create or letting the reward disturb progress. So, rewarding ourselves by playing some PlayStation is ok if we have gone to the gym as planned. Rewarding ourselves with a bag of sweets when trying to cut down on sugar is not.

Include rewards if you want to make building good habits easier. And make sure you enjoy them.

Identity & Accountability

At the core of what we do in life lies our identity. We are likely to do things that align with the person we believe we are.

> *"Do you want to know who you are? Don't ask.*
> *Act! Action will delineate and define you."*
> ~ Thomas Jefferson ~

We feel unhappy and frustrated when we do something we don't believe in. When our behaviors don't match our values and the perception of who we are, we will experience something called cognitive dissonance. There are two ways in which we can escape this feeling.

Either we change our behavior to be more in line with our values so that we still are the same person we believe we are. We maintain the same values and can now justify our actions because they align.

The other response is that we change our values instead. We change them to be more like our behavior. We change them to make it easier to justify what we do. In a way, we give up on the person we were and become a person with a different set of values.

If you are reading this book, you likely want to achieve a goal or change something. You want to change your behavior. Or you might want to change both the behavior and the person you think you are—your identity.

Changing your identity is not easy. But if you want to make it easier to achieve your goals, clearly define your core values. Define what kind of person you want to be.

"I am a healthy person. I eat well, work out, and take care of my body. All choices about health are up to me, and it's my responsibility to take care of my body. I do it because I want to and because this is who I am."

Once you have clearly defined your values and who you are, it will be easier to start acting in line with them. Then you slowly but surely begin confirming that identity. The more you behave according to those values, the stronger the new identity becomes. And the stronger the identity becomes, the more your behavior will reflect it.

You have started to become the person you want to be. And to take it one step further—if you make a public statement about who you are and what you are about to change, your chances of success will increase.

> *"A time comes when you need to stop waiting*
> *for the man you want to become and*
> *start being the man you want to be"*
> ~ Bruce Springsteen ~

If we let others follow our progress, we are likelier to follow through and make a behavior a habit. Social media platforms are excellent for making this type of public display that helps us with our own accountability. We can also try to find someone with the same or similar goals and keep each other accountable. And being part of a group trying to change dramatically increases our odds of succeeding.

Words have power, and the words we use can influence our identity. If we are trying to lose weight and eat too much sugar, we shouldn't say that we are "trying to cut down on sugar." It's better to say, "I don't eat sugar because I am a healthy person." Do you see the difference?

"No! Try not. Do. Or do not. There is no try."
~ Master Yoda ~

Have you ever noticed that when you tell someone you will try to do something, you don't really trust your own words? "Yeah, I will try to come" is not very confident. At least I have noticed it's true for me. Whenever I say I will "try" to do something, I know that the "try" means I am not all in. And then my likelihood of success is way lower. When I say I will do something, I am much surer. But even saying "I am going to" do something leaves some uncertainty. It doesn't carry the same weight as when I start doing it. Action speaks louder than words.

If there's something you want to do, why don't you do it now?

We do many things in life because we see others doing them. If others are doing it, it must be right. This is called "social proof"—when we take cues from the social environment. If no one cares about a "no parking"-sign, we don't care either. But if it's totally empty, we will not park there. Even if there's no sign telling us not to, we would still think twice if there were no cars.

Social proof is compelling when we identify as part of that group. We are social animals. We want to belong. We want to do what's considered proper and think that what others are doing must be right.

However, today we see that what most people do is not necessarily what's right or good. Just look around you. A lot of people eat junk food and drink soft drinks every day. People spend hours and hours in front of the TV. They are in constant debt and have no savings.

It's easy to follow the herd and do what they do. It's easy to fall into that trap. It's easy to go along with the 9-5 life. What's difficult is to go against the crowd. Especially when we see all our closest friends on that bandwagon.

What we *believe* others are doing might affect us more than what they actually do. We tend to believe what we see and hear in the media. It feels ok to do something when it seems everyone else is doing it.

But what the media shows is not the whole truth. Media lives on scaring people. They thrive on sensational news— horrible acts of violence, wars, disasters, and health dangers.

Advertising makes us believe other lies too. So, what we see on TV, the Internet, or read in the paper is not the whole truth. It can give us a very twisted view of reality.

When we identify as part of a group, it's simple to follow along. However, suppose we *don't* identify as part of that group. In that case, if we want to be seen as separate from them—we will probably not mimic their behavior. On the contrary, we might do the exact opposite of a group we don't want to belong to. We will *avoid* doing things that would identify us as similar to that group and might even do things that oppose them.

This is something we can use in our daily challenges. If we are tempted to buy a big bottle of Coke, we can think: "No, only fat people would do that." This reframing can help us. Or, a more general response, "No, I will not do what everyone else is doing. I am not like them."

Just make sure you can distinguish what people do in general and, what you want to do, what values you stand for. Make sure you know who you want to be, what groups you want to identify with, and what groups you don't want to identify with. Then try to act according to that.

Become great, and you will have great success.

We talked about rewards before. They can help a lot. But I have also found that doing what I believe is the right thing often is reward enough for me. I don't need to add any extra reward. The feeling I get when I do the right thing is worth more than what falling for any temptation would have been worth. My behavior confirms the kind of person I want to be, and that is sweeter than a bar of chocolate.

All that's needed is reframing the choice a little bit. So, it's not about avoiding eating chocolate. It's about doing something good for myself. It's about confirming who I am.

Progress & Success

We cannot know when we will see results. They will rarely show up right away. Therefore, it can be a good idea to display our progress in terms of effort and consistency to stay motivated. Getting a calendar where we make a cross for each day that we follow through with our tasks will make it very clear. Then we will see the progress we are making in being consistent. Our effort will be visible. A calendar has the extra benefit of also working as a visual reminder. We can put it in the bathroom, so we see it just before bedtime, in the bedroom, or in the kitchen. It depends on what we want to achieve. But it should be displayed prominently, so we can't miss it. And we should be proud. Making that cross every day is a nice reward in itself. If we make it as soon as we can after we fulfill our tasks, then the psychological reward is as immediate as possible.

If you prefer something more high-tech, get a habit-tracking app. Then you can also engage with others with the same goals.

Progress makes us proud, and it's often worth telling others about it. People might get impressed, which encourages us more. It could also confirm our identity even more if we allow ourselves to brag a bit. It makes our efforts more visible and known, giving us more to live up to. It can make us feel we have more to prove.

We keep doing this, and once the results start coming, they will often speak for themselves. We will be visibly more fit, financially better off, happier, more educated, or whatever goal we have set for ourselves.

The more public and visible the progress is, the better this works. And if you want to help others, praise them for *their* successes and battles won! Encourage them. Every little battle counts and every small battle won is worth praise.

The more we help and encourage our friends, the better they will become, and the more they will influence our own direction in life in a positive way. And the more we manage to change, the more our identity will change, and we will influence them back.

Mindfulness

Being mindful and paying attention is one of the most powerful tools for better self-control. Being present and aware of our feelings, thoughts, and body in any situation. Not judging any thoughts or feelings we have, just trying to observe and describe. Accepting it and letting it go.

In short, mindfulness is about paying more attention to what's happening here and now in our life.

Being mindful can help us in many situations in life. Studies have shown it positively affects our immune system, mood, and focus. It can also decrease stress, improve relationships, and compassion, and increase altruism. It even changes our brains and makes the grey matter in our brains denser in areas connected to learning, memory, and empathy.

So, mindfulness can be used to get all the benefits above, but it's also a tool we can use to figure out what's going on in moments we don't feel good in life.

In what situations do you not feel happy? What are you feeling? What makes you feel that way?

And, of course, it can be just as valuable to learn more about the moments when we feel good.

When we listen to our thoughts, our body, and our feelings, they can tell us when we are on the wrong path. Just as well as when we are on the right one. We just need to focus on now, not the past or the future.

Mindfulness can also help us to keep going when we are struggling. Taking a few seconds to feel and reflect can help.

What situation is it? Why am I in this situation? What am I doing? Why am I doing this? What am I feeling? Why am I feeling this? How does it feel in my body? What are my thoughts? Why am I thinking this? What are my fears? Why do I fear this?

Whenever we are tempted to take that cigarette, skip that gym session, or eat that brownie, we can stop. We can try to be more mindful. Pay attention to what's happening. Remind ourselves what the goal is—what we want to achieve. Take a little time and focus on breathing. If we need more time, we pause for a bit longer.

We always have to consider what either option will give us, what we want for ourselves, and realize we have a choice. What's the best thing we can do here and now to step in the right direction? Then we do what we must.

Willpower

To create change, we often need to force it onto our brain. We need to activate the conscious part of the brain, the prefrontal cortex, and sometimes override our current habits. We need to avoid our natural tendency to seek instant gratification. Motivation is a good friend but unreliable. It goes up and down with our current mood. Sometimes we are motivated to create change, and sometimes we are not. Sometimes we don't feel like it, or we feel more like doing something else. Maybe we want to hang out with friends, watch TV or take a nap.

> *"I don't wait for moods. You accomplish nothing if you do that."*
> ~ Michael LeBoeuf ~

So, we can't always rely on motivation. In addition, it might be high when we start changing something, but it often goes down over time. Especially if we don't see immediate results.

Imagine New Year resolutions—how many of those last longer than a month or even the first two weeks? If we really want to make a change in life, we have to rely on something else.

A more reliable friend is willpower. It influences all parts of life. People with more willpower usually have better lives— they are happier and healthier, have better relationships, have better careers, and make more money. If we want to improve life, willpower is an excellent friend.

Now I am happy to tell you that willpower has some interesting properties. The first good news is that our level of willpower is not pre-determined. Everybody has willpower, some more and some less, but it's not a pre-determined amount we have. We can build it, just like we can build muscles with training.

However, it's also limited because if we do many things that require willpower, we can run out of it temporarily. It's in limited supply in the short run, but we can increase the total amount in the long run.

We can imagine it like a gas tank that can run out. But we can train our willpower so that the tank grows and can carry more gas. We can still run out, but we will do so less frequently, and we will be able to use more willpower before that happens.

Usually, we have more willpower in the morning after a good night's sleep. Then slowly, as the day goes on and we use more and more of it, we run lower and lower on willpower.

We only have one willpower tank, which we use for all things. This is for good and bad. When we practice willpower and get more of it, it helps us in all areas where we use it.

Increasing our willpower in the gym will also help us resist temptations. But having just one tank also means using the same tank for everything we do. If we run out, we have nothing left for anything. Whenever we need to fight against an impulse, focus intensely, or do something difficult, we use willpower from that tank. And once we run out, we go into habit mode. We do what we usually do. We go back to our default settings. Whether those settings are good or bad.

If there's one thing that affects personal success, it's willpower because it helps us stay on course when facing a problem or temptation. Through willpower, we can make a behavior into a habit. So, if we work on strengthening our willpower, our habit-building efforts will become easier.

People who habitually use willpower don't even need to think about it. It has become automatic. They use their willpower to do things that are good for them and avoid the things that are not good.

So how can we increase it? Here are some ways to do that, both in the short run and the long run:

- Meditation: Even as little as five minutes every day increases our willpower.
- Exercise: Physical exercise increases our willpower. This is one of the absolute best ways to increase self-control and willpower in any area of life. And in addition, it's a keystone habit in and by itself.

- Sleep: A good night's sleep will help us with our willpower. And taking a nap will restore some of it if we run out.
- Food: Good nutrition can help increase our willpower reserve.
- Quality time with friends and family. This will help us increase our willpower reserve.
- And, of course, practicing our willpower in everyday decisions will strengthen it over time.

Everything that requires willpower will use some of what we have in the tank. Some other things that use it are:

- Big decisions: If we make a big decision, we will use some of our willpower. They seem to use the same tank.
- Sleep deprivation: If we have not slept well, we will start our day with less willpower in the tank. More of our decisions will be on autopilot, and we will need to rely more on good and bad habits.
- Stress: This is one of the biggest enemies of willpower. Stress triggers the fight-or-flight response. It directs energy from the prefrontal cortex and prepares the body to act instinctively. No deliberate action. No self-control. The best ways to reduce stress are exercise, meditation, time with friends and family, taking a walk, listening to music, reading, or something similar.

‣ Mind altered states: If we are drunk, distracted, or in any other way have an altered mind, our willpower will be weaker.

So, if we distill what we have learned so far about managing willpower, the best plan would be:

‣ Get a good night's sleep.
‣ Meditate every day.
‣ Do some exercise.
‣ Eat well.
‣ Spend time with friends and family.
‣ Avoid alcohol and drugs.

And then, we make sure to schedule all activities that require willpower in the morning. This includes the behaviors we want to make into a habit and any big decisions we need to make. This is when we have the best chance to have enough willpower in the tank.

If we want to increase our willpower long-term, we must practice it daily. Do more things that require willpower. Do more things that challenge it, so we make it stronger.

If we temporarily run out, there are a few things that can immediately boost it:

‣ First, slow the breathing to about 4-6 breaths per minute. This can calm the body, increase heart rate variability, and activate our prefrontal cortex. It puts our brain into a "pause and plan" mode instead of "fight or flight."

‣ Second, taking a walk outside, in a green area, breathing some fresh air, and we will boost our willpower.

‣ Third, relaxing—lie down, relax the body and mind, and breathe deeply. This will trigger the physiological relaxation response, lower our stress levels, and increase our willpower.

If we combine them all, we might get an even more significant effect on willpower.

For practically anything we do, if we choose the more difficult option, then we are exercising our willpower. And more willpower will help us in all areas of life.

If you want to read more about willpower and get other book recommendations, check the further reading pages at: unsucklife.net/further-reading

Taking Care of Ourselves

For optimal performance in life, we need to take care of ourselves. Our body is our machine. And our brain is the control center. Reaching our goals will be much more challenging if they don't work well. Now, this could be a book or three all by itself, so I will just go through some of the essentials superfast.

Eat

This one is not easy to do right because there are so many different opinions—vegan diet, Keto diet, slow carb diet, LCHF (Low Carb, High Fat), and even carnivore diet. I have my own personal beliefs, but I can't swear it's the best one for everyone. However, there seem to be some things that most can agree on. We should eat more vegetables and fiber. We should avoid processed foods. And we should avoid sugar in all its forms. It seems to me we should also avoid, or at least reduce, grains like wheat and corn in our diet. If you only do these things, you are eating a much better diet than the standard western diet, and you will be on your way. If we always start by eating a lot of what's good for us, we will have much less desire to eat what's bad for us.

Sleep

For adults, this means a minimum of seven hours a night. Eight is better. Nine is good. Try to sleep at night and at the same time. One of the easiest ways to get better sleep is to follow your circadian rhythm. Make sure you have a comfortable bed in a dark room, and it should preferably not be very warm. We sleep better in a slightly cold room. Avoid alcohol and avoid eating for at least three hours before bedtime. Slow down before you go to bed to make it easier to fall asleep. Reduce the lights an hour before bedtime, especially blue light from screens.

Exercise

Exercise is essential, but maybe we are not doing it right. If we look at the people who live in so-called "blue zones" — the places on Earth where people live the longest — we will see that what they do is a bit different from how we generally think of exercise. They walk a lot. They bike a lot. They work with their body. They have a lot of low intensity "training" during the day. This is quite different from sitting in front of a computer all day and then squeezing in an hour in the gym three times a week. And this is not to say that strength training is wrong. It's not. It's one of the best ways we can stay in shape. But we really need to ensure that we are more active during the whole day. We need to move more. And in addition to that, if we get some cardio and strength training, it has excellent benefits for health and longevity.

Fighting Excuses

Some people look for reasons to *do* things. Others look for excuses *not* to do things. If you feel that you might belong to the second category, read on, my friend.

I believe we have all used excuses from time to time. And we use some different ones. Of course, we don't use them with the intent to harm. There are other reasons. But they still prevent us from living a better life.

One reason behind these excuses is that we are not clear enough about what we want. Our priorities are not properly set. We are too vague in our hopes and dreams. And the biggest reason behind these excuses is probably just fear, the fear of what might happen if we do something. We don't dare to start. We are not sure we can make it or whether it will be worth the effort. We fear trying and failing. We fear others' opinions and make our decisions here and now based on what we think others expect—what we have been made to believe. We don't make decisions from love. We don't follow the heart. Strangely, we might even be afraid of succeeding. Anything that changes the status quo can be scary. So, we use these excuses to justify our behavior, but we are just fooling ourselves.

No excuse has ever taken you closer to where you want to be.

Think about that. You will not get any closer to your goal. No matter what the excuse is, it will not improve your life.

I know it's hard to change. But if we really want to achieve our goals and get the life of our dreams, then we must be clear about what we want. And we must stop making excuses.

Life can make it harder. But it almost never makes it impossible.

Here are some of the most common excuses we use. Maybe you have used some of them?

I Don't Have Time

There are so many things to do. Work is killing us. Other responsibilities are demanding. Traffic is a drag, and on and on. We feel torn between the things we really need to do, what we think we need to do, and the things we want to do.

Yes, we are often busy. But when we say, "I don't have time," what it really means is, "It's not my priority."

As strange as it sounds, the people who run three companies, take care of their kids, do voluntary work on the weekends, and are active in community groups always have time to squeeze in at least three workouts per week. They don't say they don't have time. How is that possible?

Let me ask you this: If you complain about how short of time you are, and suddenly you get another important project with a deadline—how do you solve it? Yes, somehow, you find the time. How is that possible?

Everybody has 24 hours every day. It's what we do with those hours that matters. Whatever we decide to do, we also choose not to do something else. If we don't actively decide to do something meaningful, we might passively choose to do something less meaningful. It's all about priorities.

You don't need more hours. You just need to get more out of the hours you have.

And to get more out of our lives, we must get our priorities straight and stop using excuses.

If you have 15 minutes free, what will you do?

What's preventing us from achieving our dreams? Is it that we spend our time on mindless surfing? Or maybe 3-4 hours of brain-dead TV evenings? No matter how full our day is, we can always squeeze something more in. We can always free up some time to do something meaningful.

Remember, "not enough time" is just an excuse. What do you really want in life? What do you do that you don't value much? What can you do to take yourself one step closer to your dream?

I Need Some Help

Ok, we all need help sometimes. But what prevents us from getting that help? If we really need help to achieve our dream, the first step is to get that help. If we don't know who could give us that help, we need to figure out who could. And if we have no clue about that, we need to find the person who could help us get that help. True? Saying we need help doesn't mean it's over—that it ends with that. It's just the first step toward the goal.

I Need to Learn Some More

I have used this one so many times. Over and over again. I still use it from time to time. Procrastination by preparation. So many books I had to read before feeling ready. So many things I had to learn before I could start. To do anything. And especially to write this book.

At some point, I realized I would never feel ready. It was probably fear that stopped me. Maybe fear of not finishing. Perhaps of finishing and feeling it's not good enough, or no one likes it. Or maybe even fear of finishing and succeeding because it could mean I have to change some things in life.

It can be true when we tell ourselves that we need to learn some more. Knowledge is power. I love learning. But saying that we need to know more *before we start* is a lousy excuse. We can always start. If we don't start, we will never finish for sure.

It's tricky, though. When we learn more, it feels like we are doing something. It feels like we are making some progress, but we are not. There's no action. We are not moving forward.

Being busy doesn't mean we are doing something that's improving our life or moving it in the right direction. Being active is not the same as being productive. We are not yet writing that book or learning that language. We are not making any changes.

There comes a time when we need to start doing and learning along the way. Learning by doing. We need to begin the journey. Become actively active. We need to stop giving this excuse and start taking action.

I Want to Find the Best Solution

The sister excuse for the need to learn more is the need to analyze and plan. Forever. Paralysis by analysis. Nothing will ever happen as long as we explore the options and try to find the best solution—the best way of doing something. We are not moving forward as long as we are weighing our options. We are losing time.

We can learn about potential problems and mistakes from others who walked that road before us.

Planning is needed. Planning is great. But there's planning, and then there's overplanning. There comes a time when you must start. The perfect plan doesn't exist. Unexpected things will happen, circumstances will change, and obstacles will appear. You just need a plan good enough to start. That's it.

So, we start with something. We try something that feels right. We test it out. Maybe it will not *be* right. But what if it will? Or it might be something that's "good enough." If it's not, then we can improve it little by little until it is. Before we do something, we will never know if it works. As long as we are undecided on what to do and can't pick one road and start the journey, we will stay exactly where we are.

> *"If you spend too much time thinking about a thing, you'll never get it done."*
> ~ Bruce Lee ~

Very rarely, if ever, is something perfect the first time we do it. So, we might just as well start now. Since it can take some time to start a habit, the longer we wait, the longer before we get results. It's better to start and do something.

I Would Start if it was More Realistic

It's just a crazy dream. The goal seems so far away. It will never come true. Sometimes we don't think we can make it. We don't feel we are qualified enough. We don't have the talent or the luck. Or maybe we have started but stopped because not enough has changed. The current situation is too far away from the goal.

> *"Many of life's failures are people who did not realize how close they were to success when they gave up."*
> ~ Thomas Edison ~

Sometimes we try, and we try but not much happens. And then, suddenly, it all happens at once. It's the classical "ketchup effect." You shake it and shake it. Nothing happens, and then all come at once. In life, it happens because, behind the scenes, everything is prepared. It's brewing. The compound effects are not yet visible, but below the surface, things are changing. Then suddenly, it breaks out, and everything changes in no time.

Don't think it's just a dream. Go for it, and don't stop until you get it! It might seem unrealistic, but people are already doing what you dream of, so it's possible. Maybe it was even more difficult for them than it would be for you. You never know how close you are.

I Will Start When the Time is Right

We all know it. This is a terrible excuse. Seriously.

Yes, the situation could almost always be better— financially, psychologically, or whatever. But in the end, this excuse really means we want the change, but not quite yet. That's what we are really telling ourselves. We don't like what we have now, but we will let it continue for a bit more. It doesn't sound very smart to me.

If we allow ourselves to use this excuse, it means we will never start anything because it will always be true.

It's never the "right" time. The timing could always be better. Isn't it smarter to start now and be halfway done when "the time is right"?

The best time to start something was yesterday. The second-best time to start something is today. You know it. I know it. Why wait?

*"The time is always right to
do what is right."*
~ Martin Luther King ~

I Need Some Money

Yeah, it can be challenging if there's some up-front investment to start living the dream. Money helps. But that's no reason to stop entirely. How do we get that money? Just like anything else, we take small steps forward. Start saving. It might be possible to get someone to invest. Or maybe we could even take a loan if we believe in it enough and can convince a bank about the idea.

If we decide to do it alone, how much money do we need to make every month to survive? What if we live on rice and beans? We don't need that much if we choose to start living the dream. Once again, it's about priorities. Whatever money we make *above* the bare minimum is what we can save to get the up-front investment. If we get our priorities straight, we can get the money. We can create the momentum we need. We can start living the dream with the right attitude and hard work. It requires courage. It requires sacrifices. But I believe it's worth it.

I Need to Hit Rock Bottom First

I heard this recently, and it's almost comical. This is similar to the "when the time is right" excuse but on steroids. We know things are bad. We know we need to change. But we give the excuse that it has to be even worse before we change? Seriously?

It can always get worse. So, in a way, this excuse is also foolproof. We can use it forever because we can always rationalize that we have not yet hit rock bottom.

Why would we even want to start the change from an even worse position? It doesn't make sense.

Think Why You Can—Not Why You Can't

Don't think about why you can't do something. Think why you can. Try to keep a positive mind. If you don't believe it can work, you will never start. Believe you can make it because you can. This is what starters do, what finishers do, and what winners do. Here we go again:

> *"Whether you think that you can or think*
> *that you can't, you're right!"*
> ~ Henry Ford ~

People who think this way look at the positive side. They search for reasons why they can do something. And then they do it. As long as we use excuses, the ones we have covered here seem true. Because as long as we don't do anything, it can seem like we don't have time, for example. In general, we see what we are looking for.

But as soon as we start doing, we prove to ourselves that the excuses we used before are not valid. We get a new and more positive reality. Look for reasons to do things instead of excuses not to do them.

Set Setbacks Back

If we live and experience the world on the edge of our comfort zone, we will step in shit from time to time. Maybe both literally and figuratively. We will make mistakes. We will have setbacks. It's unavoidable. Whatever we do, there's risk involved.

The best thing we can do is to just scrape it or shake it off and move on because the alternative is to never start. And if we don't, we will never experience all the beauty this world can offer.

> *"The only man who never makes a mistake is the man who never does anything."*
> ~ Theodore Roosevelt ~

Setbacks can come in many forms. We will struggle with motivation and willpower. We might fail to do what we want to do some days. Our schedules can make it nearly impossible sometimes.

Life might give us hard times, and it may turn rough for a while if we aim to make significant changes. But we need to remember that life isn't always easy. There are ups and downs. It's the downs that make us notice the ups. There's no light without darkness.

"Never confuse a single defeat with a final defeat."
~ Michael LeBoeuf ~

It's what we do when things are bad that makes the difference. If there's smooth sailing, there is no problem. But when the storm comes, that's when the sailor is put to the test. Having a setback doesn't mean it's a failure. It's temporary. Shake it off. Learn and move on.

If willpower fails you, forgive yourself and move on. Get back on track as soon as possible. Don't blame yourself. It just makes you feel bad. And when you feel bad, you are more likely to fall for temptations and fail again.

The brain will search for ways to protect our mood. The easiest way is to do just the thing we are trying to avoid—smoking, overeating, going on a shopping spree, or something similar.

Remember that nothing is perfect, but try not to fail twice a row. There will be more difficult moments—workouts that are not that good, unexpected expenses that set us back months or even years, and roadblocks on the path to our dream life. But every time we fail, we have the opportunity to learn.

It's only a failure if you give up. If you keep going, it's just a setback. And every setback is a step closer to success.

The faster we move forward, the more often we will have setbacks. The bolder the dream, the longer it might take and the more obstacles we face along the way. Success is a process. It will take time. But the faster we move, the sooner we succeed.

"If everything seems under control, you're just not going fast enough."
~ Mario Andretti ~

Imagine you will make 10 mistakes before you achieve your dream. Would you want to wait, or go slow? Or would you want to go fast, and get there sooner?

When we have a setback, we should figure out how to do it differently. What went wrong? What's the problem? How can we avoid that mistake in the future? How can we do it better? Is it time? Is it too complicated? Or is it just too hard to motivate ourselves to do it? What are the weak links? Maybe we should try to make it easier? Then we would need less motivation and willpower to follow through.

The simplest way to make it easier is to make it smaller. Another approach is to increase our ability—to get better at it, and improve with practice. Or we can search for sound advice—take a course or do something else to increase our ability. Getting better tools that make it more enjoyable can also help.

If you hesitate to do something you want to do, do it anyway. If you are bored, try to push through. Even if it's not as great as it could be. If you don't see results, remember to ask yourself if your actions are reasonable. Are you doing the right thing? If you are, keep moving in that direction. Results will come.

Sometimes it happens to me that life interrupts, and I don't have as much time to go to the gym as I would like. But more often than not, I try to go anyway, even if I would be there for just 20 minutes. It's better to do something than nothing, and it helps me keep the momentum. Especially since I need to start over again if I break the habit. When we stop, momentum dies out; instead, it works against us. We have to push harder to get started. So don't quit.

> *"What we call failure is not the falling down,*
> *but the staying down."*
> ~ Mary Pickford ~

We will sometimes be tempted not to do what we have promised ourselves. Some of those times, we will make it, but unless we have an iron will, we will most likely also have some setbacks.

To prepare ourselves for those moments, we can try to think about ways we can be tempted to break our promise. When? In what situations? What can we do to avoid those situations? And how can we stay on track if we can't avoid them? We need a plan to fight the temptations or whatever it is that can put our progress at risk. We can revise the tools that make it easier to keep a habit—maybe we can use them better. Make reminders more visible. Make the daily task a bit easier. Make rewards more attractive.

What support can we get from friends or family? Or, if we feel the temptation to break a good habit, can we distance ourselves from what's tempting us? Can we create some time or space between ourselves and this temptation? A ten-minute delay can make the brain think of it as something that lies in the future, and then it's not as tempting anymore. Or can we try to focus on our goal, pitching it against this one-time instant gratification? What do we want more?

> *"Our greatest weakness lies in giving up. The most certain way to succeed is always to try just one more time."*
> ~ Thomas Edison ~

There will be challenges, but also ways of facing those challenges. Remember that any setback or wrong decision is a chance to learn. A plane on autopilot is off its course most of the time. Still, by constantly making tiny corrections, the plane arrives at its destination in the end. It's the same with most goals in life. We will not be on course all the time. But if we learn from slips and mistakes and make sure to correct them, we will reach our goal. In addition, what we learn might be worth all the effort.

If you fall, stand up again. Try one more time. It will pay off.

Efficiency & Effectiveness

I have given a lot of praise to habits here, right? A lot of credit for doing something. Taking small steps to move forward. I believe doing something is better than doing nothing. But doing something doesn't mean we are doing the right thing or the best thing. It doesn't always mean we are moving in the best direction or doing it right.

We talked about being busy, and there are many times when we are busy but not really producing anything. And sometimes, we are doing something, but maybe not doing the right thing or doing it in the best way possible.

We need to consider two things when we evaluate what we do. One concerns efficiency and doing something right. And the other concerns effectiveness and doing the right things.

When we engage in a behavior enough times, it can become a habit. This is positive; it's what we want. But it can also be a bit negative because we stop thinking about how we can do it in a better way. It's worth considering how we do it because it might not be the most efficient way. So, from time to time, we can try to do it more consciously.

The environment might also be changing. Maybe we should quit doing something. Or there might be something else we can do that's even better. What's best to do now might not be best for all time. What was previously very effective might not be the most effective anymore.

"There is nothing so useless as doing efficiently that which should not be done at all."
~ Peter Drucker ~

So, every now and then, it's good to reflect on precisely what we are doing and how we are doing it. Is it still serving us? Is it still the best thing to do? And if it is, are we doing it the best way possible? Or can we do it in an even better way? When we combine efficiency and effectiveness, we are doing the right things in the right way.

Rings on the Water

Yet another benefit of these small actions repeated over time is that each improvement affects everything else. Getting one good habit in place can spread its effects like rings on the water.

If we are healthier, we will also be happier. When we are happier, we will think better, allowing us to work better, and in the end, we will be able to make more money. With more financial security, we can afford more time with our close ones, which makes us even happier. And then it will be easier to go and work out more often, making us even healthier. When we are healthier, we will be able to have even more giving relationships with our family and friends. And on it goes.

We face challenges better when we are well-slept, not depressed, not stressed, not malnourished, and in good physical shape. We have more willpower when we are all the above. And with more willpower, we can create better habits, which leads to more well slept, better shape, and on and on.

Every little thing we do affects us, but it also affects our friends, family, and community. What we do can spread to and influence them. And in turn, they can influence us back. Someone starts exercising and thinking about nutrition. They begin to change, get in shape, and feel better, which may inspire their partner. The partner also starts changing and manages to inspire some co-workers, which keeps it spreading.

> *"Be the change you want to see in the world."*
> ~ Mahatma Gandhi ~

Habits can affect our lives and the lives of others, and keystone habits have the most significant impact. One of the most powerful ones might be to practice willpower. It can be done in many ways, as already mentioned. Another keystone habit is exercise. The effects will ripple through many parts of life, and the positive loop will continue fueling itself. We just need to start and take advantage of the momentum to keep it going.

YOU CAN DO IT – STARTING NOW

The Time is Now

We are getting close to the end of this book. But let's play with a thought before we finish.

What if you never start? What will happen? Well, it's obvious—nothing. If you don't start whatever you want to do, you will never finish for sure. You will never reach the goal. And you will never live your dream. You would have a lot of regrets because you don't know if you would have succeeded since you never even tried.

Let's say you start in a year or two? What will happen? You would regret you didn't start earlier. Right? So, you would have regrets about that choice too.

The only way you can avoid regrets is this: Start now! I know it's possible. And if your brain is starting to invent excuses right now, stop! I know they are not valid.

Besides the regrets we can avoid, there's another good reason to start now. The results will come earlier and be greater. If we start now or start in five years, what we have in the bank ten years from now will be very different, even if we save the exact same amount each year. The money will grow for five years longer, and those five years extra make a massive difference. The sooner we start, the more we take advantage of the power of the compound effect. And this goes for practically any change we want to make. Time wasted is time lost forever. Start building on your dream now!

I Could & So Can You

If you are reading this, it means I achieved my goal. Not the goal of you reading this, but of me finishing writing this book. I needed to write it. It was something I had never done, and therefore quite scary, but also something I really wanted to do. I thought people like me would find value in it and believed it was something I could complete. So, I decided to do it. And I did.

I admit it was a struggle sometimes. I have used several of the excuses I write about. The one I used most was that I needed to learn more. I used it more the more I wrote. Mission creep. I wanted to feel that I had covered what I wanted to cover, even if I didn't even know what it was. I just kept discovering more.

I managed to avoid some of the other excuses I have written about. I did everything myself, which made it faster. So, I didn't excuse myself because I needed help. I haven't let anyone else proofread it, for example. And since I am not a native English speaker, you might have found some mistakes or strangely built sentences (sorry). I am also very aware that I have written it, on purpose, in a more conversational style. It's not always grammatically correct. But I think I get my point across.

The biggest struggle was that it took way longer than I hoped it would—mostly because I didn't make it a habit at first. Once it was a habit, it was fast since I kept writing and progressed a little daily.

I am still struggling as I write this—I feel a bit unsure. Is it good enough? Does it make sense? Will people read it? But I have realized it's just something we must accept—we will always have doubts.

Anyway, since you are reading this, it means I dared to go ahead and publish it. If I could achieve something I had never done before, something as big as writing a book, so can you.

So, what do you really want to do? Or what do you want to change? Do you believe you have what it takes? Do you really want it bad enough? Try to be specific. Why do you really want this? Can you break it down into small behaviors that will lead to your goal? Can you make habits out of those? What's the concrete plan? How will you do this? When will you do it? Where will you do it?

> *"Know that anything is possible as long as you keep working at it and don't back down."*
>
> ~ Eminem ~

Whatever you want to change, it's as simple as that. I guess more than 50 percent of people never take the first step, and 90 percent of those who start will not keep going. That's the difference. Are you among the 95 percent who will stay where they are, or are you among the five percent who will make it?

Life is hard. It's hard to go to the gym five times a week. But it's also hard to walk up the stairs if you weigh 150 kilos. It's hard to save money. But it's also hard to pay the bills when you are poor. We just have to choose in what way we want life to be hard.

Remember, achieving the change you want is not the end. You need to keep going. There's a reason the change happened. If you stop doing what made the difference, you will soon be back where you started. Don't stop!

"The future belongs to those who believe in the beauty of their dreams"
~ Eleanor Roosevelt ~

Once again, let's play that game: Imagine you are on your last day in your life, and you meet the person you could have been. I mean the person you would be if you followed all your dreams. How would it feel? What would that person look like? How would that person behave? What would that person have done in life? What would their memories be? How would they feel about life?

Are you on a path to becoming that person? Or are you on a different path? And most importantly—what do you need to start doing now to be that person in the end? Remember, you are the one in charge. Do what you have to do right now to give yourself what you deserve in the future. If you do it, you will be that person in the end. The one who feels happy about life.

Last Words

I believe in all I have written here, but I still don't follow it all. I still struggle with some of it, but the changes I have made so far have helped me greatly. And they will continue to help me. The more changes I manage to go through with, the better it will become.

I really hope it will help you too. Even if it doesn't lead to a total life transformation, I hope it will give you inspiration. I hope it will change the way you think, maybe make you exercise a bit more, or try to get more willpower, and hopefully, some change in the habits you keep. I hope you will start following a bit closer to your dreams—not living only for other people. Follow your heart a little bit more.

If it does lead to some change, I am thrilled! Please, feel free to tell me in what way it has inspired or changed your life. Just email me at kristofer@unsucklife.net, or write it in a review.

Also, feel free to visit the site and social media accounts for the book:

- unsucklife.net
- facebook.com/unsucklife
- youtube.com/@unsucklife
- tiktok.com/@unsucklife
- pinterest.com/unsucklife
- instagram.com/unsucklifenow
- twitter.com/unsucklifcnow

We talk about the same topics as in the book—there will be new texts, more ideas, and maybe new tools to help change people's lives. And who knows, perhaps I will post your story after you make that change!

One of the best ways to keep up is to sign up for the newsletter:

- unsucklife.net/newsletter

And if you want tips on other books that have inspired me, find them on the further reading page at:

- unsucklife.net/further-reading

If you know someone else who might not be living their dream life. Someone who is not following their heart or has a passion that they are not exploring enough. Someone who might need to stop smoking, fix their finances, lose some weight, start working out or follow that dream. Someone you believe could change their life for the better if they got a bit of a kick in the ass. Then please help them too! Talk to them about what I have written here. Or send them a link to get the book. Help them stop living the lies. Push them in the right direction. Encourage them.

Change is contagious. When we change any aspect of our life for the better, someone close may also start changing. Bad physical health is contagious, but so is good. Negativity is contagious, but so is positivity. Help each other move forward. Overcome the obstacles. Inspire other people. Become an example.

Whatever change you seek, your successes will help you, and theirs will help you.

I believe the more people live happy, healthy, and fulfilling lives, the better this world is. Life is fantastic, and I think it can get even better!

So, when do you start? If you start tomorrow, you lose one day. If you start in a month, you lose one month. If you start next year, you lose a year. At any moment, you can decide to change your life forever.

"So many of our dreams at first seem impossible, then they seem improbable, and then, when we summon the will, they soon become inevitable."
~ Christopher Reeve ~

You know the kind of life you have and the kind of life you want. Finish this, and then do something that brings you one step closer! Do something good for yourself. Not just thinking or planning. Act. It's never too late. Good luck! Take care of yourself. And remember:

Just one small step.

Now.

Printed in Great Britain
by Amazon